Getting
to the
Heart
of
Friendships

AMY BAKER

Getting to the Heart of Friendships

by Amy Baker

Cover Design by Christina Marsh

ISBN 13: 978-1-885904-87-4
ISBN 10: 1-885904-87-8

PRINTED IN THE UNITED STATES OF AMERICA
BY
FOCUS PUBLISHING
Bemidji, Minnesota

To Jeff
My beloved

With Grateful Thanks

To Jeff, my wonderful husband who never complained when I left on weekends to spend hours at the office.

To Rob Green, who took the time to read this manuscript and offer big picture comments. He also checked to make sure my theology was correct.

To Steve Viars, who pushed us to write. I'm sure I wouldn't have started this project without his leadership.

To Elyse Fitzpatrick and Martha Peace, who said they believed I could write and provided encouragement in the process.

To Janet Aucoin, who wanted the women's retreat on friendship to be solid and meaty.

To Jerry Jamison, who agreed to edit the manuscript on short notice and who signed his comments, "Your approval, control, protection, rightness, pleasure, comfort, and prestige-oriented friend."

To Jan Haley, who has represented Christ so well throughout the publication process.

To Mrs. Mixon, Mrs. Cryan, Mrs. Viars, and Mrs. Jamison, you've been role models for me of godly women for many years.

To Terri Culp, who is truly a genuine friend.

To my family, whom I love.

To the many others who have blessed my life and encouraged me to have God as my best friend.

Table of Contents

Chapter 1
We Were Made for Relationships
But Our Friendships Often End in Fiasco

Two of my earliest best friends were girls I'll call Christy and Brittany. We became friends early in grade school and our friendship continued into junior high. I remember sleep-overs at Brittany's house and my delight when I was invited to Christy's fifth grade birthday party. I still have the party favor Christy gave to everyone who came.

In 8th grade, Brittany suggested to me that we should ignore Christy, because Christy was getting "stuck up." Although I hadn't noticed that Christy was stuck up, I sinfully followed Brittany's suggestion and stopped talking to Christy in the lunch line. I shamefully abandoned my friendship with Christy. Soon, Christy started hanging out with new friends and no longer tried to be friends with Brittany and me. Shortly after that, Brittany crossed me off her friendship list, and I was left with no friends.

What went wrong? These girls had been my friends for years! How could our friendships be so easily destroyed? Why weren't we lifelong friends?

I wanted friends, but something went awry in a major way. You can chalk it up to the fact that I was a junior high school girl, or you can look deeper. I followed Brittany's suggestion because it seemed like the easiest thing to do. I cared little about being a genuine and authentic friend; I cared a lot about what was easiest for me.

Perhaps like me, you have friendship stories you wouldn't be proud to share. Perhaps like me, you've had more than one friendship fiasco. Perhaps you'd like to get to the heart of friendships.

We Long for Relationships

I love the *Anne of Green Gables* movies. Recently, after several months of trying to keep pace with a demanding schedule, I scheduled a weekend with no commitments, just to rest. I decided to make it an *Anne of Green Gables* weekend, and I watched the entire set of DVDs—over 10 hours of *Anne of Green Gables*. It was a wonderful weekend.

If you love Anne's story as I do, then you know how she longs for a bosom friend. Many of us can relate to Anne's desire. As she expresses her desire for a bosom friend to Marilla, her longing resonates with us. And perhaps one of the reasons it touches us is because Anne's desire is our desire as well. We long for Anne to have a bosom friend, and we long for a bosom friend of our own.

We Were Made for Relationships

We long for relationships because we were created for relationships. God made this clear from the beginning when He declared it was *not good* for man to be alone. Up to this point, everything about God's creation had been good. What else would you expect from an imaginative Creator who could paint the sky blue, cause the wind to whisper on a sun-drenched orchard, and fashion man out of nothing? And this creation was judged to be a winner, not by some talent show judge, but by the One with flawless taste and exquisite judgment. The One who is the perfect critic.

Very good, no corrections needed. The ears don't have to be redone because they're a bit lopsided, the tongue isn't too long to fit behind the teeth, the kneecap isn't backwards, and the fingernails are on the tops of the fingers, not the bottom. This creation is not only good, it's very good!

Surprisingly, however, something is not good. It's not good for man to be alone. And before there is time for the critics to offer their analysis of how to make it better, just like that—it's fixed. God created woman. God created a bosom friend for Adam.

Now God lets Adam be the creation judge. How will Eve fare? Will she be harshly dismissed or invited to remain? The universe waits to hear Adam's evaluation.

Adam is blown away. He can't believe how good Eve is. He gives her the highest accolade in his vocabulary—she's like me! God created the perfect bosom friend for Adam.

These two best friends had something else going for them. Not only were they created by God, Adam and Eve were created in God's image. God, who Himself exists in perfect relationship in the Trinity—one God—the Father, Son, and Spirit who function in perfect unity, perfect harmony, perfect relationship, and perfect friendship.

It gets better! God desired to have a relationship with Adam and Eve. He communicated with them personally and directly. God didn't send Adam text messages from heaven. He communicated with Adam face to face. God is for relationships. I mean, He's really for relationships.

We're Tempted to Use Relationships for What They Will Do for Us

If God is for relationships, then why do I have friendship fiascos? When I look at what I long for and what I've got, where is the disconnect? Here is what happened. When Adam and Eve made the choice to sin, their decision affected us all. Since that time, every one of us has made the same decision; we've all chosen to sin. And those choices have created one friendship fiasco after another.

In their book, *Relationships: A Mess Worth Making*, Timothy Lane & Paul Tripp make this statement:

> "We enter relationships for personal pleasure, self-actual-ization, and fun. We want low personal cost and high self-defined returns."[1]

---

[1] Lane, Tim & Tripp, Paul, *Relationships: A Mess Worth Making* (Greensboro, NC: New Growth Press, 2006), p. 48.

What do you think about that statement? I think what Lane and Tripp say has a lot of truth in it. Herein lies the problem. I wasn't created to use relationships for what they will do for me, and God didn't create you to live for yourself. Any time we try to function in a way that God didn't design us to function, things get messed up, and that usually involves relationships.

Suppose I told you I was sending you a certificate via the mail for a free blender. You eagerly check the mailbox for the next several days, anticipating the arrival of the certificate. On Wednesday, it comes. You tear open the envelope and the certificate drops out, along with a page of conditions to redeem the certificate.

Among the usual provisions such as expiration date, you find this rather odd restriction: "The giver of this certificate requires the user to chop a cord of wood into kindling in the blender before any other use of this product." With a provision like that, would you grab your car keys and head to your nearest Wal-Mart to get the blender?

Probably not. But why? Because we both know that if you tried to use the blender to chop wood, the blades would break, the motor would overheat, and the blender wouldn't work. It would be a waste of your time to redeem the certificate for a product that would break on its first use. In fact, this example seems ludicrous. Who would ever try to chop wood in a blender? The blender wasn't designed to chop wood. Trying to use the appliance in a way that it wasn't designed to function will certainly lead to failure. The blender will break.

We get this. What we often don't get is that the same is true for us. When we try to function in a way God didn't design us to function, it doesn't work. Life gets hard; there is frustration, anxiety, and depression; and relationships become dysfunctional. It is ridiculous to try to function in a way God didn't design us to function and expect it to work. Isaiah 1:28 spells it out explicitly: *"Rebels and sinners will both be broken, and those who forsake the LORD will perish."*

Is There Hope?

When Satan was successful in tempting Adam and Eve to sin, the picture became bleak. God can't look upon sin with favor; He is disgusted by it.

Having a good relationship with someone who is disgusted by us is next to impossible. Sin scuttled our relationship with God.

Not only was our relationship with God scuttled, our relationships with each other were torpedoed as well. In just a few short chapters into the Bible, relationships have become so bad that murder is reported. A far cry from the friendships and relationships God designed us to have.

But in His mercy and grace, God didn't allow Himself to be ruled by His disgust for our sin. God loved us. Even when we'd become His enemy, God loved us. In love, God sent His Son to pay the penalty for our sin, for our selfishness, and for our shameful abandonment of our relationship with Him.

Through His death on the cross, Christ reopened the doors to sweet relationships, first of all with God Himself and then with each other. When we confess our sin—our failure to function as God designed us to function—and trust in Christ for salvation, God becomes our Father. A sweet relationship is established with God. Additionally, God sends His Spirit to live in us, enabling us to function the way we were truly created to function.

So, How Were We Created to Function?

Why were we put on Earth? Suppose we were to say to God, "You put me here, now what do you want me to do?" If He replied, "Love the Lord your God with all your heart and with all your soul and with all your mind. … and love your neighbor as yourself," what would you think about His purpose in creating you? Would you think that you were created to be your own god? Would you think that you were created to live for your personal pleasure, self-actualization, and fun? Would you infer that you were created to live for yourself?

You might have inferred that you were created to live for yourself if God had said, "The greatest command is this: Make sure no one hurts you; that no one looks down on you; that you take care of yourself; that you're never dependent on anyone; and that no one tries to fit you into their mold. Be your own kind of person." But God didn't command you to be your own kind of person. If you are honest with His command, you would infer that God created you to love and worship Him and to love and serve others. To fulfill these commands demands that we establish relationships with God and others. In fact, we could probably say that fulfilling these commands defines true friendship. We are friends with God when we love Him with all our heart, soul, and mind. We are friends with others when we love them as ourselves.

God makes it pretty clear that He didn't create us to make up our own rules. When Lucifer attempted a heavenly coup, God didn't go into committee and review the proposal for its merits. Satan was cast out of heaven and all his mutinous crew with him. God didn't put us here to live for ourselves, to make up the rules, or to be our own god.

Perhaps you were taught long ago that you were to live to glorify God. You've been able to quote 1 Corinthians 10:31 since first grade, when you memorized it in Sunday school. *"Whether you eat or drink or whatever you do, do it all for the glory of God."* But somehow, you've never fully understood how that applies to friendships. It's important that we study how to glorify God in our friendships so that we don't default to inauthentic relationships.

What is your default orientation in pursuing friendships? We all have one. Perhaps your default orientation has been to get approval. You've used your friends to get their acceptance and left them feeling smothered.

Perhaps your default orientation in friendships has been control. You've wanted to be the ruler in your relationships, and your goal has been to have friends who will do what you say.

Maybe the default orientation in your friendships has been protection. You enter friendships on the alert for any signs that your friend will hurt you. When the signs appear, you desert the friendship like a frightened rabbit bolting for cover.

For some, the default orientation of friendships is "rightness," in which you are the judge who wants everyone around you to live by your standards and your rules. Your friends don't experience grace and mercy at your hands; they are expected to rigidly conform to your rules.

On the other hand, you may have very little interest in following the rules or in having friends who follow the rules; your orientation in friendships is pleasure. Friendship is all about having fun. You are not concerned about being a friend who helps those in her friendship circle get to a better place. For you, friendship is all about living it up.

Perhaps your default orientation in friendships has been comfort. You are willing to offer friendship to anyone as long as it's convenient, but you are reluctant to exert effort and quick to ditch relationships that require hard work.

Maybe you've used friendships to gain prestige. Individuals are only accepted as friends if they are part of the "in" group. Outsiders need not apply; they are not welcome in your circle of friends.

All of these orientations are deficient when it comes to being a genuine and authentic friend. Each orientation primarily centers not on God's glory but on one's own desires.

If, instead of worshiping God and serving others, we choose to function as if God put us here to please ourselves and make up our own rules, what might we expect to happen? We should expect relationships to become dysfunctional—just like a blender used to chop wood becomes dysfunctional.

The sweet thing is that the friendships that blossom from a pure heart deliver everything Anne of Green Gables expressed in her desire for a bosom friend. Friendships which blossom from a pure heart reflect the love, joy, and unity of the Father, Son, and Holy Spirit.

I want that. I assume you want that. The critical component here is the heart. Sweet friendships aren't simply a result of applying a few biblical principles to relationships in the hope that we will profit from their application. Getting friendships right goes deeper than actions. It has to reach all the way to the motives of our heart.

Why? What makes the motives of our heart so important? We'll examine this more thoroughly in chapter two.

Chapter 2
What Makes the Heart So Important in Friendships?

When Anne of Green Gables expresses her desire for a bosom friend, I've never paused the DVD and said; "Now I wonder what Anne's motive is for wanting a bosom friend?" I've never paused the DVD, but God would. In Jeremiah 17:10 God says, *"I the LORD search the heart and examine the mind, to reward a man according to his conduct, according to what his deeds deserve."*

Why would God do that? Why would He search the heart and examine the mind? Because your heart is the wellspring of life (Proverbs 4:23). What does that mean? What is a wellspring? A wellspring is the source or supply of something. Thus, if the heart is the wellspring of life, it is the source of your life—your control center. In other words, everything you do comes from your heart.

Our Hearts Direct Everything in our Lives

When the Bible talks about your heart, it's not referring to the organ that pumps blood, it's referring to your control center. (This is probably what we would refer to as our *mind*.) Your heart is intricately involved in every decision you make, every word you speak, and every act you perform. Not so sure about that? Would you believe it if Christ said it? In Luke 6:45 Christ said this: *"The good man brings good things out of the good stored up in his heart, and the evil man brings evil things out of the evil stored up in his heart. For out of the overflow of his heart his mouth speaks."*

It's impossible to have friendships that aren't directed by the heart. And it's impossible to have genuine, authentic friendships if what is stored in our heart is self-centered and self-absorbed. Bad hearts produce bad friendships. Good hearts produce good friendships.

Your heart is central to every friendship you develop. If you want good friendships, if you want friendships that are genuine and authentic, you have to have a good heart. There isn't any alternate route. God doesn't work like a GPS in which you punch in your destination and then get to choose the shortest time, shortest miles, or the newest freeways. God sets the course, and His route goes through the heart. God will not be mocked; any attempt to detour and ignore the heart will lead to destruction. You will arrive at the end of your route and find loneliness, alienation, and despair. Following God's route and going through the heart is crucial.

So, How Do I Develop a Good Heart?

How do you develop a good heart? Do you want the bad news or the good news? Let's start with the bad news and get it over. You can't develop a good heart. I can't! Well, then, why am I reading this book?! Remember, there is good news, too.

You see, you can't develop a good heart because the heart is beyond cure. God lays out our terminal condition very plainly. He doesn't try to sugarcoat it and lead us to believe that if we go through chemotherapy we'll be cured. He's honest. Our heart is beyond cure. To see His specific diagnosis, look at Jeremiah 17:9: *"The heart is deceitful above all things and beyond cure. Who can understand it?"*

Beyond cure. That's discouraging. Yes, but wait until you hear the good news! Here's the good news. You can't develop a good heart, but God can give you a new heart. Ezekiel 36:26-27 gives us a résumé of God's capabilities in this area.

I will give you a new heart and put a new spirit in you; I will remove from you your heart of stone and give you a heart of flesh. And I will put my Spirit in you and move you to follow my decrees and be careful to keep my laws.

While the book of Ezekiel is clearly addressed to the Israelites, God is certainly capable of giving a new heart to anyone. He's not limited in His practice or only capable of giving a new heart to the Jews. God is the Great Physician. He's able to give a new heart to anyone! (And the New Testament makes it clear that He's still doing heart surgery.)

In the 1960's a fierce competition was taking place between a handful of surgeons to make history by performing the first human heart transplant. Although these surgeons filled out no official entry forms, never took their places in the starting line, and never heard the loud report of the starting gun, the race was more intense than any Olympic competition.[2] These surgeons were passionate about what they were doing because they understood the desperate neediness of their patients.

Patients who are put on the list for a heart transplant are on a death march. There is no cure for their condition. Our condition is beyond cure as well. We, too, desperately need new hearts. And that is what God offers as we trust in Christ. His Spirit comes to live within us.

Suppose your physical heart is beyond cure and you need a transplant. As you spend your time on the list of those waiting for a donor, you daydream about the type of donor heart you'd like to receive—a heart like that of Olympic medalist swimmer Michael Phelps, football quarterback Peyton Manning, or Boston marathon winner Salina Kosgei. Imagine your joy after a successful transplant if your surgeon announced to you that the heart you received was from a world class athlete.

Now consider the heart transplant offered by God; not the physical organ, but the control center, the wellspring, of your life. Remember, you are desperately needy. There is no cure for your condition. What donor would you secretly daydream about for this transplant? Whom would

---

[2] Chris Barnard of South Africa crossed the finish line first on Dec. 3, 1967 when he transplanted the heart of Denise Darvell into Louis Washkansky. McRae, Donald, *Every Second Counts: The Race to Transplant the First Human Heart,* (New York: G. P. Putnam's Sons, 2006).

you choose—the mind of Albert Einstein, Abraham Lincoln, Winston Churchill, Thomas Jefferson, Madame Curie?

How stunning if your surgeon announced that the "heart" (mind or control center) you are to receive is the Holy Spirit. Wow! The very Spirit of God living in you. That's better than Albert Einstein, Abraham Lincoln, Winston Churchill, Thomas Jefferson, and Madame Curie all put together. Incredibly, that is the new heart God offers! When we trust Christ as our Savior and Lord, the Holy Spirit comes to live in us.

This is good news since, as we saw in Luke 6:45, the good man brings good things out of the good stored up in his heart, and the evil man brings evil things out of the evil stored up in his heart. You can't get a better heart than the heart of the Holy Spirit. Think of all the good that can come out of that heart. Now it's possible to have genuine, authentic friendships!!!

Is That All There Is to It? Get a New Heart and All My Relationships Get Fixed?

No, that's not the way it works. God says we have to discipline ourselves to godliness. We have to train ourselves to use the new heart.

Prior to having the heart transplant of the Holy Spirit, no amount of discipline would have created a good heart. Oh, perhaps we might have had some days that were better than others. But like a patient with a diseased physical heart who tries to climb a mountain, success isn't possible. Maybe on good days the heart patient can get out of bed and make it to a chair, but she would be foolish to think she'll ever scale a mountain. And ultimately, her bad heart will kill her.

Similarly, without the Holy Spirit we might have days that are better than others; we're kinder, less annoyed, or more patient. But we'll never be able to climb the summit of pleasing God with any success. Without the work of the Holy Spirit in our lives, it's impossible to please God. Our attempts will be no more successful in reaching the goal than the efforts of a heart patient would be in climbing Mount Fuji.

A heart transplant changes all that. Now we can be like Kelly Perkins, a heart transplant recipient who has climbed a number of mountains since receiving a heart transplant in 1995, including Mount Fuji, Mount

Kilimanjaro, and the Matterhorn. Did Perkins leave the hospital after her transplant and immediately set up base camp? Of course not. Will we immediately have genuine, authentic friendships when the Holy Spirit takes up residence in us? No. As with the physical heart transplant, there will be rigorous training, exercise, and conditioning. But it's possible!

Can You Imagine the Mountains You Might Conquer with a New Heart?

Maybe your mountain is overcoming living for the approval of others. Perhaps all your life you've been enslaved to the fear of man. You've been afraid of what others will think of you. You've asked your friends whether they're upset with you so often that they're tired of hearing it. You're ashamed to admit it but your desire for approval has resulted in participating in activities you're against—sex outside of marriage, drugs, or drunkenness.

With your old heart, genuine, authentic friendship wasn't attainable. Perhaps you could have altered your behavior a bit. For example, when you found out that your friends were tired of always being asked, "Are you mad at me?" you might have learned to ask that question less frequently. But what would have motivated you to ask less frequently? Winning their approval! Your heart is still diseased. Your heart is still oriented toward getting approval. All you've done is found an improved method for pursuing your idol of approval.

Bad hearts tear up friendships. Have you ever been disrespected by one of your friends? Ridiculed? Dumped when someone "better" appeared? Backstabbed? Used? Gossiped about? Ignored? All those sins can wreak havoc on friendships. Worse, have you ever treated any of your friends this way? Sin puts us on the fast track to alienation, living without true friendship in an existence of aching loneliness.

The gift of a good heart means we can build friendships that are genuine and authentic. Friendships built on a right foundation bring joy and gratification. The next chapter unveils the beginning steps of the building process we want to undertake.

Chapter 3
Preparing the Site: Friendship Orientations

Math is not my strong suit (I still count on my fingers), and civil engineering is so far beyond my cognitive abilities that I think it would be easier for me to walk to the moon than grasp the principles that builders use. However, I have learned this. You must build on a proper foundation. If you don't, whatever you build on top of the foundation will eventually crumble. When this happens, it's devastating.

I've also learned that in some building projects, it is necessary to clear away rubble before the building can begin. If you're going to build a 5-Star resort, you will bulldoze any shacks currently standing on the property. A 5-Star resort owner wouldn't want any part of the resort to be less than exquisite, so anything that would detract from a 5-star experience is ruthlessly eliminated.

As we begin to construct genuine, authentic friendships, we too may need to begin with demolition. Any impediment in our hearts that would result in defective or deficient friendships needs to be bulldozed.

Like a resort property owner who goes over every square foot of his property, we need to thoroughly examine our hearts. To provide a 5-Star resort experience, no thistle is allowed on the resort golf course, no termites are tolerated in a guest bungalow, and no beer bottles are left scattered on the beach. Likewise, in our hearts, personal idols should be pulled up by the roots, selfish ambition should not be tolerated, and ungodly philosophies should be hauled to the dumpster.

In the next seven chapters, we're going to bring in a demolition team and seek to implode friendship orientations that stand like shacks on resort property. To pretend a shack is a luxury suite is self-deceptive. Shacks on resort property are demolished, not photographed for billboard ads. Likewise, to pretend that any of the friendship orientations we're going to visit in the next seven chapters represent true friendship is self-deceptive.

The orientations we'll see in the coming chapters are a way we can examine how we approach friendships. These friendship orientations are caricatures, not rigid personality types. However, because God says that all of us have hearts that are prone to go astray, I suspect you may see aspects of yourself in some of these orientations. In reality, most of us are probably a blend of several orientations. I saw aspects of myself in all of them.

I've tried to define key distinguishing features for the various orientations to make the task of looking into the heart easier. We may display some of these features and not others. The traits may be present to a small degree, or they may be a ruling disposition. My desire is that to whatever extent we see characteristics of these orientations lodged within our hearts, we'll profit from the self-examination and find new ways to grow in Christ's likeness.

To the degree that these characteristics are present, our friendships become less genuine. No longer oriented toward loving God and loving others, we become dominated by a love of self. The inauthentic friendships we're going to consider include:

> The person who uses friends to gain acceptance: an **approval-oriented friend.**

> The person who uses friends to exercise power: a **control-oriented friend.**

The person who looks for friends who won't ever hurt her: a **protection-oriented friend.**

The person who expects others to live by her standards and rules: a **rightness-oriented friend.**

The person who is all about living it up: a **pleasure-oriented friend.**

The person who just wants life to be easy: a **comfort-oriented friend.**

The person who wants to be part of the "in" group: a **prestige-oriented friend.**

All these orientations are deficient when it comes to being a genuine and authentic friend. Each orientation primarily centers not on God's glory, but on one's own desires. In other words, as Lane and Tripp said, we end up entering relationships "for personal pleasure, self-actualization, and fun. We want low personal cost and high self-defined returns."[3]

When demolition experts implode a building, they carefully target where to place their explosives in order to achieve the best result. Following the lead of Lane and Tripp,[4] we're going to target five areas as key to imploding inauthentic friendships.

The first three areas address the inner man; the last two areas address the outer man. We've already discussed why the inner man, or the heart, is so important. The heart is the source of our behavior. However, it's not always easy to get a clear view of the heart. First Corinthians 2:11 points out that no man knows another man's heart. Thus, it is difficult to know the motives and desires of another. Not only that, but it can be difficult to know our own hearts. Proverbs 16:2 indicates that we all tend to believe the best about ourselves; however, according to Jeremiah 17:9 we may simply be deceiving ourselves because the heart is deceitful above all things and beyond cure.

---

[3] Lane, Tim & Tripp, Paul, *Relationships: A Mess Worth Making* (Greensboro, NC: New Growth Press, 2006), p. 48.

[4] In their book, *Relationships: A Mess Worth Making,* Lane and Tripp chart some typical patterns in friendships when it's about me. I'm indebted to them for the foundation they've poured in their excellent book. I'll use their chart as a springboard in considering how relationships might go wrong.

Thus, given the difficulty of discerning the heart, it can be helpful to examine the fruit produced by the heart, or in other words, the outward behavior and actions brought forth from the heart. If bad fruit is present, this can be an indicator that a bad heart is present. If good fruit is present, this can be a sign that the underlying heart is pure.

Finally, relationships don't occur in a vacuum. At least two people must be involved in order for a relationship to exist. If we are to love our neighbors as ourselves, we surely have to consider the effect our actions and behaviors have on others.

Our five key areas are as follows:

1) Our *heart's desire* in each friendship. For each friendship orientation, we want to discern what rules our heart in our friendships. Could the ruling motive be approval? Control? Prestige? What are we seeking in friendship? What do we want? Remember, we act out of our hearts. Thus, anything that occurs in any friendship stems from our heart.

2) The *acceptable cost* in order to get what we want in friendship. What are we willing to pay (in relationship terms) in order to achieve our heart's desire? What will we sacrifice? Are we willing to give up intimacy? Are we willing to give up problem solving? Are we willing to give up authenticity? What will we pay?

3) What are our *biggest nightmares or fears* in our friendships? Do we fear loss of power, loss of approval, loss of ease? What are our dislikes or pet peeves?

4) What does our friendship orientation look like when *seen in action*? What kind of fruit is evident when the desire of our heart is approval? What kind of fruit is evident when our heart's desire is protection?

5) What will the friendship experience be like for those who develop a friendship with us? What do *others experience* in our friendship? Will they feel manipulated? Will they feel used? How will they be tempted to respond to us?

Why go to all this work? Why seek to get to the heart of friendships, especially when it could be painful? Because what God offers is immeasurably better than cheap imitations. Have you ever purchased a designer knock-off piece of jewelry or handbag only to have it disintegrate during its first use? When you purchased the product it sure looked genuine, but upon using it you discovered the truth of the adage, "you get what you pay for." You're left with a product that is useless, and you're frustrated over being taken in by a cheap imitation.

Any friendship not rooted in loving God and loving others is a cheap knockoff. It may look like the real thing until you test it out. Then you discover your friendship isn't genuine, it isn't authentic. When put to the test, the friendship unravels and you're left with alienation, loneliness, and estrangement.

On the other hand, when we understand the incomparable joy of genuine friendship, any pain necessary to achieve it becomes inconsequential. Suppose Publisher's Clearing House showed up at your door to announce you'd just won $1 million. If you stubbed your toe on your way to answer the doorbell would you blame the people at the door because they caused you to stub your toe? Hardly! Even though the pain of your stubbed toe is real, the joy of your prize overshadows the pain. Paul expresses this concept in Romans 8:18; suffering fades when we consider the outcome.[5]

So let's get started. Let's begin the process by examining the approval-oriented friendship.

---

[5] Romans 8:18: I consider that our present sufferings are not worth comparing with the glory that will be revealed in us.

Chapter 4
The Approval-Oriented Friend
Friends Who Long for Acceptance from Others

If you had told me before I married my husband, "Jeff is planning to ask you to marry him," I would have considered you a good friend for bringing me such wonderful news. If I lost something that cost me a lot of money, and, without waiting to be asked for help, you told me where to find my lost stuff, I would consider you a friend. If I wanted to hire you to provide a service for me, and you provided it free of charge, I would consider you a friend. If you saved the best T-bone steak on the platter for me, or if you threw a party for me when I got a promotion, I would consider you a friend. If I was going through a Senate confirmation hearing in which I faced opposition, and you were able to persuade everyone to confirm my seat, I would consider you my friend. If you could show me when and how I could overcome my opponent, I would consider you a friend.

Heart's Desire

The Old Testament Prophet Samuel was this kind of friend to Israel's first king, Saul. Samuel brought Saul the good news that he would be king (1 Samuel 9 & 10). Samuel told Saul his lost donkeys were found (1 Samuel 9:20). Samuel provided his services to Saul for no fee, when Saul expected to be charged (1 Samuel 9:7, 20). Samuel served Saul a special portion of meat he had saved for him (1 Samuel 9:23-24), and he made Saul the guest of honor at a banquet for 30 people the day before Saul learned he was to be king (1 Samuel 9:22). Samuel reaffirmed Saul's appointment to the throne when some of the Israelites voiced opposition to Saul as king (1 Samuel 10:27, 11:14). Samuel gave Saul the battle plan from God to eradicate his enemies, the Amalekites (1 Samuel 15:1-3).

Samuel was a great friend to Saul. He was a great friend, not because they were chums, not because they played golf every Friday, and not because they moved in the same social circles; Samuel was a great friend to Saul because he served Saul and had Saul's best interests at heart. Samuel wanted Saul to follow God. Clearly, this would benefit Saul. God had made it clear to the Israelites long ago that if they followed Him they would experience unparalleled blessing. On the other hand, if the Israelites forsook God, destruction would surely follow.

Samuel wanted what would be best for Saul. Nevertheless, Saul ignored the instructions Samuel gave him from God. Saul showed no respect for his friend Samuel (or God). The disintegration of Samuel's friendship with Saul is recorded in 1 Samuel 15.

When Samuel was alerted by God to what his friend had done, he went to talk to Saul. Saul had the nerve, even after disrespecting Samuel in such a major way, to greet Samuel as if everything was okay. Saul then lied to Samuel to his face. When it became clear that Samuel already knew the truth, Saul gave him an excuse that to an approval-oriented friend seemed the equivalent of an ironclad alibi, *"I was afraid of the people and so I gave in to them."*

When Saul's excuse didn't seem to work with Samuel, Saul resorted to begging. He begged for Samuel to remain his friend. He was so desperate that he grasped Samuel's clothes in a frantic effort to keep him from leaving and ending their friendship. Undeterred, Samuel kept going and his robe tore in Saul's hands.

Saul begged for one more act of friendship. This act of friendship was so important to him that even though Samuel had made it abundantly clear their friendship was over, Saul persisted. "Honor me before [everyone else]." In other words, "Please help me to keep the approval of everyone else." How pathetic! What a sad end to a friendship.

Like Saul, the heart of the approval-oriented friend is controlled by a desire for acceptance and approval. It is very important to the approval-oriented friend for others to like her. Her friendships revolve around receiving acceptance and being approved.

Nightmare/Fear

A friend who longs for approval from others fears being rejected, not being accepted, or being disliked. We see a tragic example of this in John 12:42-43:

> *Yet at the same time many even among the leaders believed in him. But because of the Pharisees they would not confess their faith for fear they would be put out of the synagogue; for they loved praise from men more than praise from God.*

Here are people who craved praise from men more than praise from God. Think about the implications of this choice. They were willing to give up praise from:

- The One who has more wealth than Bill Gates.
- The One who has more power than the American president.
- The One who is smarter than Nobel Prize winners Watson & Crick who pieced together the puzzle of DNA.
- The One who is more beautiful than anyone who struts down a Hollywood red carpet.

These leaders essentially said, "I want the friendship of people God created more than the friendship of the Creator." While these words may never have been spoken aloud, these sentiments controlled the hearts of the leaders in John 12. Similarly, the approval-oriented friend fears being rejected by people and is willing to give up the approval of God.

Acceptable Cost

Those who seek approval from their friendships are willing to make sacrifices and pay high costs. Approval-oriented friends are willing to be controlled by anyone who can provide approval. Often they will follow the crowd and do whatever it takes to fit in. If that means engaging in drinking, drugs, and sex, the approval-oriented friend is willing to pay that price.

This is not necessarily always the crowd the approval-oriented friend follows. At times, the most attractive friends from whom to seek approval will be Christians. Friendship with Christians may seem especially attractive since Christians often have more peaceful relationships than those who don't know Christ. Christians often have relationships that aren't marked by conflict.

Since the approval-oriented friend fears conflict and the possible rejection conflict might bring, she may be motivated to follow a crowd of Christians and imitate their activities. Sadly, however, the eternal outcome may be worse than if she were to follow the crowd in drinking, drugs, and sex.

How could that be? Here's how. The approval-oriented friend who seeks the approval of Christians will join in church-related activities. Because she always agrees with those around her and is reluctant to express an opinion, those around her may come to believe she has trusted Christ as her Savior and believe she has a genuine relationship with our Wonderful Lord. Alas, her relationship with God is a fake, but because she followed a Christian crowd, rather than a crowd caught up in ungodly activities, no one may see the need to discuss her relationship with God with her.

God, however, doesn't judge us by the crowd we hang out with but by the heart. God knows if her profession was only made to please others. If so, she is in danger of hearing the pronouncement made in Matthew 7:21-23. *"I never knew you. Away from me, you evildoers!"* Lamentably, the cost of gaining approval by following the Christian crowd may be eternal separation from God—receiving His disapproval for eternity with no recourse to receive His favor or approbation.

No matter what group of friends the approval-oriented friend chooses, she will rarely communicate to solve problems. Communicating to solve problems risks having her friends get upset. Thus, she will sweep problems under the rug. She is willing to pay the price of living with unsolved problems. It matters little if problems fester and result in harm for her or her friends. In fact, she is willing to overlook almost anything, rather than risk having her friends upset with her. She will let you drive drunk, give a presentation with broccoli stuck in your front teeth, divorce your spouse, gossip about your boss, cheat on your taxes, scream at your kids, browbeat everyone around you, and ruin every friendship you have—without saying a word. Although she may know the instruction in Ephesians 4:25-26 to solve problems quickly so that Satan is not given a foothold, she is not concerned about this. Solving problems seems too dangerous if she might lose the approval of friends.

Seen in Action

Perhaps it would be helpful to walk through a typical day of a friend who longs for approval, looking at how her orientation is seen in action.

6:30 am   The alarm rings, and Sophie wakes up with a knot in the pit of her stomach. What will she wear today? Yesterday she wore a dress to the office. At lunch, all her friends were wearing pants. Sophie was afraid her friends thought she was overdressed. She would wear pants today, but she has an appointment with a wealthy, elderly client who always wears dresses. If she wears pants, Sophie is afraid she'll offend her client, but if she wears a dress, Sophie worries what her lunch buddies will think of her. Maybe she could wear a dress and change into pants before lunch.

8:23 am   While commuting to work, Sophie gets a text message from her friend Amanda asking her to tell their boss that she is sick today and won't be in. Amanda tells Sophie in her text that she's going shopping with her sister. Sophie is afraid that if she tells Amanda that she doesn't want to lie to their employer, Amanda won't like her. Sophie shuts her phone off so she can pretend she didn't get the message.

11:59 am Sophie looks at her watch. It's almost time for lunch. She starts worrying about her clothes again.

12:02 pm Sophie sees her lunch buddies, Chastity, Holly, and Greta, waiting in their normal spot and heads in their direction. She sees Greta looking at her dress and knows Greta thinks she's overdressed again.

Sophie reaches the little group just as Chastity states that it is Sophie's turn to pick where they eat. Sophie immediately says, "I don't care. Where would you like to go?" After several rounds of "I don't care where we eat. Where would *you* like to go?" Greta suggests they go across the street to Panera. Relieved the decision is made, but certain Greta is mad at her, Sophie trails behind the lunch buddies into Panera.

Inside the eatery Sophie asks Holly, "What are you going to get?" When Holly responds that she's not sure, but she thinks she'll get soup, Sophie asks Chastity what she's getting. Chastity has already decided on the New England clam chowder, and Greta is in line for the broccoli cheddar soup. Sophie really wanted a chicken Panini, but she's afraid that if she gets a sandwich everyone will think she's a pig. Instead she orders chicken noodle soup.

12:53 pm   Sophie stands and takes all the soup bowls, utensils, cups, and napkins to the trash. When Holly comes back from the restroom and sees everyone's ready to go, she runs to the counter to get another iced tea. Sophie realizes that she threw Holly's cup away, and now Holly can't get a free refill. "Holly, I'm so sorry! I shouldn't have thrown your cup away. Let me pay for the tea. Are you mad at me?"

1:15 pm   Back at her desk, Sophie is convinced Holly is angry that she threw away her cup, even though Holly assured Sophie it was no big deal.

5:15 pm   Sophie shoves her key in her front door lock and twists the key hurriedly. Dropping her purse by the door, she races up the steps to get ready for the game night at Hannah's house. Sophie hasn't had a night at home for six weeks, but she was afraid Hannah would be mad if she told her she needed to stay home and do laundry.

6:06 pm   Sophie rings Hannah's doorbell wondering if she's too early. Hannah said 6:00 but maybe she expected everyone to be fashionably late. Maybe Sophie should have waited another half hour. Sophie wonders if Hannah will be upset with her.

6:15 pm   Hannah doesn't seem to be upset. She smiled when she opened the door, and Sophie has listened carefully to any inflections in Hannah's voice to detect if she is irritated by her early arrival.

6:16 pm   Sophie tells Hannah she has a beautiful home. "I could never do anything that looked this good. You should be on HGTV. Your house is nicer than any of the stuff I've seen their designers do. You should be an interior designer," Sophie gushes.

7:18 pm   Mike wanders out of Hannah's kitchen with a plate of dessert in his hand. As he takes a bite of the Mississippi Mud Cake Sophie brought he asks, "Who made the cake?" Sophie's stomach lurches. "He doesn't like it," Sophie determines.

But when Hannah replies that Sophie made the cake and asks him, "Isn't it good?" Mike enthusiastically agrees as he takes another mouthful.

"I didn't think it turned out very well. It's not as moist as it should be," Sophie responds deprecatingly.

7:32 pm   The group gathered around Hannah's dining room table decides to play Uno. Since Sophie has never played Uno before, Vic quickly explains how to play.

When Sophie discards a *Draw 4 Wild Card* on her first turn, someone mentions that the rules say you can only play the *Draw 4 Wild Card* if you don't have any other cards you can play. Vic had forgotten to explain about the wilds cards, nevertheless, Sophie apologizes profusely. She is certain everyone must be upset with her.

11:15 pm   Sophie lies in bed wondering whether Amanda will be mad at her tomorrow for not responding to her text.

Perhaps you have friends like Sophie. Perhaps you *are* Sophie. If you are an approval-oriented friend, you probably display some of the following characteristics. Let's list the characteristics and then consider what God thinks of such characteristics.

•   <u>You are fearful</u>. You are continuously worried about what others are thinking of you. Although you try to hide it, you may still appear anxious and needy. This may increase if you sense others are rejecting you.

God's opinion of this: You are acting like a pagan.[6] Pagans are always worried about what's going to happen to them. You ought to fear Me rather than people. I can send both body and soul to hell;[7] none of your friends have that kind of power.

- <u>You don't solve problems</u>. When you are upset, you tend to clam up. You don't express disapproval because you fear loss of your friendship.

  God's opinion of this: You are giving the devil a foothold. When you don't solve problems, and you let issues remain unsolved day after day, you give Satan the opportunity to sow seeds of bitterness.[8]

- <u>You hide your true thoughts</u>. You are reluctant to express an opinion to your friend without first knowing your friend's opinion. You habitually try to find out what your friend's opinion is and then agree with her.

  God's opinion of this: You are not being open and transparent. By failing to be open and transparent, you are deceitful. In essence, you are lying when you simply tell others what you think they want to hear. I detest lying lips.[9]

- <u>You work hard with the wrong motive</u>. You try to earn approval by inexhaustibly serving others.

  God's opinion of this: Serving others is a good thing. However, if you serve with wrong motives, it will profit you nothing.[10]

---

[6] Matthew 6:26, 27, and 32: Look at the birds of the air; they do not sow or reap or store away in barns, and yet your heavenly Father feeds them. Are you not much more valuable than they? Who of you by worrying can add a single hour to his life? For the pagans run after all these things, and your heavenly Father knows that you need them.

[7] Matthew 10:28: Do not be afraid of those who kill the body but cannot kill the soul. Rather, be afraid of the One who can destroy both soul and body in hell.

[8] Ephesians 4:26-27: "In your anger do not sin": Do not let the sun go down while you are still angry, and do not give the devil a foothold.

[9] Proverbs 12:22: The LORD detests lying lips, but he delights in men who are truthful.

[10] 1 Corinthians 13:3: If I give all I possess to the poor and surrender my body to the flames, but have not love, I gain nothing.

- <u>You don't believe the best</u>. You believe the worst about others. If someone doesn't greet you, you believe it's because she's upset with you. If someone doesn't call, you believe it's because she's angry. If someone doesn't praise your dessert, you believe he didn't like it. If someone doesn't smile when you tell her your idea, you believe she thinks your idea is bad. You are very sensitive to the facial expressions, voice inflections, and body language of others. You draw conclusions based on these observations, and you are certain you know what others are thinking.

  God's opinion of this: You are unloving. Love believes the best. You are assuming the worst.[11] While giving attention to the facial expressions, tones, and body language of others may give you clues about what someone is thinking, you should never draw conclusions on these things alone because you cannot know what another person is thinking unless he communicates it to you.[12]

- <u>You over-commit</u>. Because saying "no" might result in someone's displeasure, you will agree to any obligation, even if it means you can't responsibly fulfill your current obligations.

  God's opinion of this: You are seeking man's approval rather than my approval. When you pursue man's approval in place of my approval, you are not my servant and I am not pleased.[13]

- <u>You practice flattery and insincerity</u>. You frequently flatter others to gain friends. You give insincere or overblown praise.

  God's opinion of this: Flatterers are hateful.[14]

- <u>You seek affirmation from others</u>. You put yourself down in hopes that others will disagree. You continuously test the waters to see if others approve of you.

---

[11] 1 Corinthians 13:7: It always protects, always trusts, always hopes, always perseveres.

[12] 1 Corinthians 2:11: For who among men knows the thoughts of a man except the man's spirit within him? In the same way no one knows the thoughts of God except the Spirit of God.

[13] Galatians 1:10: Am I now trying to win the approval of men, or of God? Or am I trying to please men? If I were still trying to please men, I would not be a servant of Christ.

[14] Proverbs 29:5: Whoever flatters his neighbor is spreading a net for his feet.

God's opinion of this: You are seeking your own honor.[15]

What Others Experience

What is it like to be friends with someone who longs for approval? Does this friendship provide the joy, unity, and communion enjoyed by the Father, Son, and Holy Spirit?

We wouldn't expect a rotted orange tree to produce sweet, luscious oranges. Nor can we expect that a rotten heart's desire will produce sweet, luscious friendships. No bad tree bears good fruit. The friendship experience with an approval-oriented friend will turn sour.

If you become a friend of someone with a heart that yearns for approval, you may experience the following:

<u>Your initial experience may be enjoyable</u>.

Initially, it may seem that friendship with an approval-oriented friend will be sweet. In the beginning it's probably enjoyable because it is nice to have someone who wants to please you, who builds you up, and who doesn't confront you. Sadly, for some, this type of friendship can go on for years, without causing distress. Neither party recognizes the friendship isn't genuine or authentic.

Some friendship orientations may be especially susceptible to the inauthenticity of an approval-oriented friendship. Perhaps the most vulnerable is the friend who loves to be in charge. The friend who wants to be in charge loves approval-oriented friends, because they allow her to always take control.

While the control-oriented friend may be most susceptible to a long term inauthentic relationship, it's easy to see that many would be attracted to an approval-oriented friend. For those who desire truly genuine friendships, a relationship with an approval-oriented friend will not be satisfactory on a long term basis. The following features may contribute to the friendship turning sour.

---

[15] Proverbs 25:27: It is not good to eat too much honey, nor is it honorable to seek one's own honor.

<u>Your friend requires constant reassurance from you.</u>

One of the disquieting features of friendship with an approval-oriented friend is that you are continuously questioned as to whether you're upset with her. As your friendship grows, you realize you are always being asked, "Are you mad at me?" or "Are you upset with me?" You wonder what you've done to cause your friend to ask such questions. You haven't communicated dissatisfaction. You're not upset. You find out, however, that you didn't greet her, or you failed to smile, or you didn't sit next to her at a social function. Perhaps you looked at your friend and said nothing at all. Perhaps your friend just "sensed" something wasn't right.

A friend who longs for approval forces you to continuously reassure her that you like her, that you're not mad at her, that you want her around. Much of your energy in group gatherings can be absorbed in making sure she feels included. You may feel exasperated that, rather than assuming that you invited her because you want to include her, she forces you to offer reassurances and coax her into participating by assuring her that you want her to be part of the group. You wish you didn't have to reassure her so often.

<u>Your attempts to give helpful instruction are unsuccessful. Your friend hates correction.</u>

If you seek to give your approval-oriented friend helpful instruction, she assumes you are expressing disapproval and displeasure. She will respond by apologizing profusely and believing you are mad at her.

Because she is so devastated by correction and assumes this means she is not liked, you may be tempted to let her continue in harmful or sinful practices. It's easier not to correct her, than to point out helpful changes and then spend two weeks trying to convince her you are not mad at her.

<u>You only get to know the person your friend wants to portray.</u>

When you ask for her opinion, your approval-oriented friend won't tell you. Instead, she'll seek to learn your opinion so she can agree with you. It's unlikely that you will know if she disagrees with you. She won't tell you.

It is difficult to know whether the beliefs of an approval-oriented friend are genuine or not. She may profess to know Christ as her Savior but her profession may simply be an attempt to conform and to please people. The approval-oriented friend may tempt you to believe she is a Christ-follower when she really is not. Because she agrees with you, commits to any service opportunities presented, and imitates your choices, you may believe she wants to glorify God. In reality, she may only want to please you.

<u>You come to believe your sin is not that bad.</u>

Your approval-oriented friend never helps you get to a better place or to grow. Because she never confronts you about sinful practices, you may be encouraged to believe your sinful choices are no big deal. Being friends with an approval-oriented friend sets you up for greater disapproval and correction from God.

<u>You let your friend who longs for approval do the serving, rather than sharing the load.</u>

The approval-oriented friend may tempt you to allow her to do all the serving while you pursue pleasure and comfort. Rather than helping you become a servant like Christ (John 15), she encourages you to be selfish.

Clearly the approval-oriented friend is not functioning the way God intended in her friendships. She does not love God with all her heart, mind, and strength, nor does she love others. The approval-oriented friend actually loves herself.

Chapter 5
The Control-Oriented Friend
Friends Who Want to Be in Charge

I grew up the middle child of the three daughters born to my parents. My sister Molly was eight years older than I, and I loved having her as a big sister. Molly was good to me, and I wanted to be like Molly when I grew up. As a teenager, Molly liked Coke and pizza, and, although I didn't like either Coke or pizza as a child, I was sure that when I got to be a teenager like Molly, I would like both. I wanted to be just like Molly.

This desire led to my decision to go to the same college Molly attended and led to considering the same major. I love Molly and am proud to be her sister.

My sister Pam was a year younger than I. Because we were so close in age we were playmates growing up, and I couldn't have asked for a better little sister. Pam was always loyal to me, and excited when good things happened to me. I remember that Pam and her second grade friends would run over to wave and say hi when our fourth grade class passed them on the playground on our way to a school activity.

In the high school I attended, homecoming queen candidates were nominated by the school's extra-curricular organizations. I happened to be a member of a club that met to elect their candidate toward the end of the nomination period. By that time, all the obvious candidates had been nominated by other clubs. Because there were no other available nominees, I was nominated as the homecoming queen candidate for that particular club.

During homecoming week, the entire school had a rally at which all the nominees were introduced. As each name was read, the candidate's friends clapped and cheered. Knowing that I was the least-likely-to-win candidate, I anticipated that the announcement of my name would be greeted with silence. Yet when I was introduced, my sister Pam jumped to her feet and cheered wildly for me, regardless of what others might think of her.

I love Pam. Having her as one of my best friends has been wonderful. Nobody could ask for better sisters than Molly and Pam.

Our parents' names were Virgil and Mary, but imagine if my dad's name had been Laban and we'd been born several hundred years earlier. Suppose that in those days of arranged marriages, our dad had married both Pam and me to the same man. Suppose also that both Pam and I were control-oriented in our friendship. Imagine what might have happened.

Not much imagination is needed if you're familiar with Genesis 29-30 and the story of Rachel and Leah. After their father Laban married both these sisters to the same man, a control war erupted in a major way for the supremacy with their husband.

Both Rachel and Leah believed they could win the war by providing sons for their husband. Each was convinced that providing children for her husband was the secret to having control. As a result, rather than treating each other as beloved sisters, they acted as competitors, vying for their husband's love and honor. Their husband Jacob was treated as nothing more than a boy toy, and Rachel and Leah argued over who got to sleep with him (Genesis 30:14-16). Each wanted to have the upper hand over her sister.

Leah took the lead early in the child bearing race, giving birth to four sons. Not to be outdone, Rachel twice asked Jacob to father a child for her through her maid servant, Bilhah. When her maid bore a second son, Rachel crowed, *"I have had a great struggle with my sister, and I have won!"* (Genesis 30:7). God ultimately opened Rachel's womb (Genesis 30:22) and she gave birth to Jacob's youngest—and favorite—son, Joseph.

It is no wonder that the sons these sisters raised hated their brother Joseph and conspired to murder him. Looking at the lives of these two women, it's easy to see the devastating results of control-oriented friendships.

Heart's Desire

The heart of the friend who wants to be in charge is consumed with the desire to have power and control. The friendships of a control-oriented friend are centered on having others do what she wants. She accepts you as a friend only if you do what she says. Like Rachel and Leah, relationships become very competitive. In fact, it's sometimes difficult to recognize these relationships as friendships at all. The relationship might be better described as winner/loser; ruler/subject; master/servant; or bully/victim.

Nightmare/Fear

Losing the upper hand is the control-oriented friend's biggest nightmare. From the perspective of a friend who wants to be in charge, lack of control amounts to defeat. She experiences loss of control as keenly as any team who gets thrashed by their opponent. Loss of the upper hand devastates the control-oriented friend.

Frequently, control-oriented friends fear being seen as dependent or needy. They are unlikely to acknowledge when they need help because this would be a sign of weakness. However, this is not always the case. Some control-oriented friends are willing to be seen as helpless and wounded because they use this to manipulate others. This type of friend doesn't want others to see her as independent or competent, because that would put her at risk of not being able to control others through helplessness.

No matter what control strategy she employs, a friend who loves to be in charge will jealously guard her control, fearful that she may lose it. She may withhold information, approval, praise, or affection to keep her friends under her thumb.

Acceptable Cost

Those who are control-oriented pay a high price for this orientation. Often, control in friendships is won at the cost of genuineness and warmth.

The control-oriented friend probably knows little about "phileo" or brotherly love. To the friend who loves to be in charge, having power over people seems sweeter than the warmth and intimacy associated with brotherly love. Controlling the remote is better than allowing your best friend to watch her favorite TV show. Bending the will of your friend to your own seems better than tender affection. Eating at your favorite restaurant seems better than seeing your friend relish a Sonic burger. Having the upper hand seems better than fellowship. Like Rachel and Leah, controlling your husband seems sweeter than love.

How sad to live for control when God's word clearly tells us:

- We can't turn one hair on our head white or black (Matthew 5:36).

- We can't make the rain fall or the sun shine (Jeremiah 14:22).

- We can't add a single hour to our lives (Acts 17:24-28).

- We can do nothing apart from God (John 15:5).

- We can't make the sun rise one minute earlier or cause it to set one minute later (Isaiah 45:7).

- We don't even know what will happen tomorrow (Proverbs 27:1).

- Any power we possess comes from God and He can take it back whenever He wants (John 19:11).

- Anything we do is in vain unless God is involved (Psalm 127:1, 2).

- The only thing we can control is ourselves and even that is a gift of God and fruit of the Spirit (1 Corinthians 4:7, Galatians 5:22-23).

- We can seek to control all we want, but what happens is up to God (Proverbs 16:9).

In her quest for supremacy, this friend doesn't want others to take the lead, to receive honor that she hasn't been given, or to own possessions that are considered superior to her possessions. The control-oriented friend covets these things for herself. She gives up contentment and lives with jealousy and self-pity if deprived of these desires. These emotions are acceptable to the control-oriented friend because she believes she is entitled to them if things don't go the way she wishes. It's ironic, isn't it, that living for control often results in being controlled—controlled by ugly emotions.

Seen in Action

As we did in the previous chapter, let's walk through a typical day again, this time with a control-oriented friend.

7:30 am   Victoria sees Debra's minivan pulling into the driveway as she finishes tying the laces on her walking shoes. Both Victoria and Debra want to develop a habit of exercising regularly and have agreed they can encourage each other. Their plan is to walk by themselves during the week and together every Saturday morning. On Saturdays, they will walk for five miles at Victoria's favorite park. Since it's on the way, Debra has stopped by to pick up Victoria.

Victoria functions as a back seat driver all the way to the park, informing Debra of the shortest route, alerting her to potholes, and pointing out when the cars ahead of them start to brake. When Debra begins to pull into a parking space at the park, Victoria insists that they take a spot much closer to the walking trail. "For pity sake," thinks Debra, "we came to get some exercise. Why can't we walk across the parking lot?" With a resigned sigh, however, Debra reverses and pulls into the spot six spaces closer to the walking trail.

After three times around the 1.25 mile trail that encircles the pond, Debra tells Victoria that she's going to have to quit because her knee is really bothering her. "You can't desert me now," Victoria pleads. "Just go a little longer."

Debra explains that she'll wait in the van until Victoria finishes, but she's afraid she'll damage her knee if she keeps going. Victoria angrily responds, "Whatever. It's all about you, isn't it" as she stalks off for her final lap. Victoria purposely takes her time, wanting Debra to have to wait and hoping she will feel bad for quitting. On the way home, Victoria does her best to make Debra feel guilty for leaving her to walk alone.

9:30 am   Victoria finishes making her list of people to ask to serve at the Crisis Pregnancy Center banquet. Each person on the list is someone Victoria has helped in the past. She is confident they all will feel like they owe her and won't turn down her request.

9:31 am   Victoria dials Natalie's number. When Natalie answers, Victoria requests her help for the upcoming banquet. Natalie tells Victoria she'd love to help, but she promised her neighbor she'd help her plant her garden that night.

Victoria responds, "But this is more important than planting the garden. You can plant the garden anytime. Your neighbor will understand. I thought we were friends."

When Natalie doesn't give in, Victoria hangs up the phone seething. Mentally she moves Natalie to her group of blacklisted friends.

9:39 am   Victoria next dials Jillian. After explaining why she's calling, Victoria manipulatively states, "Natalie says she won't help, but you're not going to let me down, are you? I know you're always there for me."

10:32 am   Victoria finishes calls to eight more people. She asks them to serve at the banquet, subtly reminding them of how she has helped them in the past.

11:15 am   Victoria runs to the grocery store to get some fresh lobster for the dinner party she's having this evening. Last week, Marcia and Tim had Victoria and her husband, Dane, over for dessert. Victoria has returned the invitation by inviting them to dinner. She plans to serve lobster bisque, prime rib, fresh green beans in soy sauce, Waldorf salad, homemade yeast rolls, and raspberry truffle cheesecake.

11:18 am   In the seafood department, Victoria sees Candice. Spying steak in Candice's cart, Victoria asks if she is celebrating something special. Candice responds that she and her husband have invited their neighbors over for a cook-out. Victoria immediately feels a twinge of jealousy. "You told me you guys weren't doing anything this weekend," Victoria accuses.

12:30 pm Dane walks in from the garage holding Victoria's car keys in his hand. Victoria regularly leaves her keys in the ignition, even though Dane has asked her not to do this.

"Honey, what can I do to help you remember not to leave your keys in the ignition?" Dane asks nicely.

"I don't see what the big deal is. The car is in the garage, it's not like I leave the keys in the ignition when the car is parked on the street," Victoria replies, irritated. "If you loved me, you wouldn't care if I leave them in the ignition."

3:27 pm Victoria calls to talk to her stepson, Cameron. Dane told Victoria yesterday that Cameron has decided to go to Disney World this summer with his mother (Dane's former wife) rather than to the Wisconsin Dells with Victoria and Dane. Although Dane is not upset by Cameron's decision, Victoria is. She tells Cameron she doesn't understand how he could do this to his dad, especially after everything Dane has done for him.

5:20 pm Victoria asks her husband to set the table for her. When he's done she readjusts all the silverware and water glasses, instructing Dane as she does so on the proper way to set the table.

6:52 pm Marcia and Tim want to know if Victoria and Dane are going to sign up for the co-ed volleyball league again this fall. Tim comments that Victoria should have gotten the award for 'most competitive' last season, noting that Victoria was even more aggressive than the guys on the team.

7:53 pm Marcia suggests the two couples get together next weekend and go to a movie. Victoria immediately responds with what she thinks is a better idea, "Let's go to that Shakespeare in the Park play I saw advertised in the Leisure section of the Post Tribune. I can call and get tickets for us tomorrow," she volunteers. She ignores the disappointed expression on Marcia's face.

10:45 pm   Coming to bed shortly after Dane, Victoria fumes that he has the remote control to their bedroom TV. Dane is clearly enjoying the Weather Channel's three day forecast. Victoria flounces and turns on her side with her back to Dane, miffed that she can't watch the news.

Perhaps you have friends like Victoria. Perhaps you *are* Victoria. If you are a control-oriented friend, you probably display some of the following characteristics. Let's list the characteristics and consider what God thinks of them.

- <u>You try to manipulate by making your friends feel bad or by using guilt</u>. You make statements such as, "Don't you care that …" or "If you loved me …" You hope that by making your friends feel bad, you can get them to do what you want.

  God's opinion of this: You want your desires to be the standard your friends use in making decisions. I want people to live by the truth of My Word. My Word tells you what is right, and it gives joy to the heart (Psalm 19:8). When you try to manipulate others to live by their feelings, you are actively going against me.

- <u>You try to manipulate by eliciting sympathy</u>. You are willing to portray yourself as helpless, hurting, frightened, or wounded. You may try to win sympathy and control through tears or even threatening suicide.

  God's opinion of this: You are actively trying to tempt people to see themselves as your source of comfort and your rescuer. You are tempting them to believe that you would be harmed if they don't intervene. You are leading them to believe that your salvation and well being is dependent on them.

  I am the True Comforter, the One who is the source of all comfort, but you tempt your friends to believe you receive your comfort from them. Once they believe this, they become your slave, because if they were to desert you, you have led them to believe you would have no comfort or hope. You are exploiting their mercy for your selfish ends.

- <u>You try to manipulate by giving or withholding affection</u>. You subtly exert pressure by refusing to smile or greet others warmly when you are trying to get them in line. You give those who don't submit to you the 'cold shoulder.'

  God's opinion of this: I want you to love others (Matthew 22:39) and you are callously disobeying my command. You are selfishly looking out for only your interests (Philippians 2:3-4).

- <u>You become angry when you don't get your way</u>. You use your anger to intimidate others. You make sly jabs at whoever has incurred your displeasure.

  God's opinion of this: You are cruel. I thought I made this clear in Proverbs 27:4 when I said, *"Anger is cruel..."*

- <u>You want others to be in your debt</u>. You don't want to be in anyone's debt. You want to always be able to call in favors; you never want to be put in a position where others can call in markers from you.

  God's opinion of this: You understand Proverbs 22:7 that the borrower is servant to the lender and that the rich rule over the poor. So you've decided you want to be able to rule by not owing anyone anything (money, favors, service, etc.) However, you have ignored my instruction in Romans 13:8: *"Let no debt remain outstanding, except the continuing debt to love one another, for he who loves his fellowman has fulfilled the law."* You should never stamp "paid in full" on that obligation.

- <u>You want undivided loyalty from your friends</u>. You don't want your friends to be tight with anyone except you.

  God's opinion of this: You are like Diotrophes, who loved to be first (3 John 9-10). Diotophes wanted everyone to be loyal to him. He wickedly gossiped in order to try to discredit others and when that didn't work he refused to show kindness to new people and blackballed anyone who did accept or show kindness to new folks.

- <u>If being nice doesn't get results, you stop being nice</u>. If you can't get people to comply by being nice, you resort to threats. You want everyone to be submissive to you.

  God's opinion of this: If I told masters not to threaten their slaves, do you think I'll be okay with you threatening your friends (Ephesians 6)? I am opposed to you throwing your weight around and lording it over others. Instead, you are to submit to others out of reverence for Christ (Ephesians 5:21).

- <u>You withhold good</u>. You withhold information or help in order to retain control. You don't teach others how to do something so they will be dependent on you. When traveling in a group, you don't make maps for every driver; they must follow your lead car. You offer to purchase tickets so you can distribute them and control seating.

  God's opinion of this: It is wrong for you to withhold good from others.[16] I don't withhold good (Psalm 84:11, Matthew 5:45). You are to be perfect in this quality, as I am perfect (Matthew 5:48).

- <u>You have to win</u>. You are competitive. You don't know how to play for fun or let someone else win. It's not fun unless you win.

  God's opinion of this: You are really the biggest loser. Whoever wants to be first will be last.[17]

What Others Experience

The joy, unity, and communion enjoyed by the Father, Son, and Spirit are strikingly absent for friends of those with a control orientation. When control is the idol of the heart, companions will be seen as objects to be dominated, not loved ones to be enjoyed and served. Friendship with a friend who loves to be in charge may hold the promise of being linked to power, but the result is not peace and security, it is turmoil and discord.

<u>Your initial experience may be enjoyable</u>.

---

[16] Proverbs 3:27: Do not withhold good from those who deserve it, when it is in your power to act.

[17] Matthew 20:16: "So the last will be first, and the first will be last."

The control-oriented friend may initially stir up your admiration, gratitude, or compassion. She may seem to be capable and competent. She may take the initiative to reach out to you when you have a need. She may achieve a lot. Her team is often the winner. Friendship seems attractive.

Or, you may feel sympathetic toward your control-oriented friend because she seems to carry a heavy burden. She may gain your sympathy because she has physical or emotional burdens. You may initially reach out in love and enjoy serving her.

The approval-oriented friend will enjoy friendship with a control-oriented friend because the approval-oriented friend is willing to sacrifice control to gain approval. Since the control-oriented friend wants control, these two may believe they have found a bosom friend. The protection-oriented friend may initially feel safe with the control-oriented friend, because the control-oriented friend seems to exercise control over others. The comfort-oriented friend may initially enjoy the control-oriented friend because the control-oriented friend is willing to take charge and organize, allowing the comfort-oriented friend to enjoy her ease. None of these friendships are authentic.

You feel like you owe something.

The control-oriented friend is adept at subtly reminding you that you are in her debt. You feel like you are always in hock to her for a loan you didn't even realize you were making. Like the naive borrower who visits a loan shark, you learn that favors done for you by a control-oriented friend have a huge interest rate. You are expected to give her your undivided loyalty and service. If you don't pay on time, she sends out her "collection agents" of anger, ostracization, guilt, and manipulation. Thus, you feel compelled to buckle under to your control-oriented friend because of favors she has performed for you in the past.

You often feel guilty.

The control-oriented friend may often manipulate by using guilt. If you don't submit to her control, she may insinuate that you won't grant her request because you don't love her or care about her. You find you give in even when you don't think you should.

If you try to talk to your control-oriented friend about problems, it always seems to turn into a conversation about how you need to change. You may often walk away from discussions feeling guilty. You may give up on confronting your friend who loves to be in charge or abandon solving problems with her. Over time you may acquiesce. You may jump to do her bidding.

<u>You feel like your ideas or decisions are never good enough</u>.

When someone offers a suggestion, the friend who loves to be in charge normally offers what she says is a better way to do things. If you suggest sending a birthday card, she'll suggest calling and singing Happy Birthday; if you suggest an after-church fellowship at your house, she'll suggest that someone else's house is closer. Sooner or later you will be tempted to give up offering suggestions because your friend won't allow herself to be outdone. You no longer follow the command in Hebrews 10:24 to consider how to spur one another on toward love and good deeds. Every time you try, you get outdone. It's easier to let your control-oriented friend do all the 'considering,' since your ideas are always rejected.

<u>You never get to lead, you are expected to follow</u>.

Because leading would indicate you are in control, the control-oriented friend doesn't allow you to lead. Your place is to follow. The title role belongs to her, and you dare not steal the show.

<u>You may feel intimidated</u>.

Associating with a control-oriented friend can be intimidating. The control-oriented friend sometimes uses anger to gain compliance. You may be afraid of her anger and reluctant to cross her. She frequently has a "my-way-or-the-highway" attitude.

<u>You may follow her example</u>.

You may be tempted to believe manipulation is an effective way to get what you want. Watching your control-oriented friend in action, you may be tempted to believe your desires can be satisfied by subjugating others.

<u>You may become exclusive in your friendships</u>.

Your control-oriented friend will not be happy if you form friendships with others that either exclude her or are stronger than your friendship with her. This presents a threat to your friend who loves to be in charge, as she fears losing your loyalty and service. Thus, your control-oriented friend may be very jealous of any outside friendships you develop.

She may try to weaken or destroy friendships you have with anyone other than herself. She will do this by 'badmouthing' you to your friend, badmouthing your friend to you, creating schedule conflicts in which you are forced to show loyalty to one friend or another, threatening to end her friendship with you and to remove any advantages associated with it, or any other ploy she can devise to rein you in.

Proverbs 27:4 notes, *"anger is cruel and fury overwhelming,"* and then asks, *"but who can stand before jealousy?"* Sadly, the friends of someone with a control orientation see Proverbs 27:4 in action as they feel beaten down by her jealous grasping for dominance. It's very difficult to stand before jealousy. Thus, when she applies measures to cow you into submission, they will often be effective. You may begin to look to your control-oriented friend for all your friendship needs. You may also begin to believe exclusivity in friendships is a sign of love and friendship.

Control-oriented friends lead lonely lives. Few of the people they call friends genuinely love them. In the end, the price of gaining control is loss of relationship. This friend loves herself, not God and others.

Chapter 6
The Protection-Oriented Friend
Friends Who Don't Want to Be Hurt in Relationships

Imagine, if it was possible, wandering around a 1st century graveyard reading the grave markers of the early church.

Jesus Christ
He is not here, He is risen.

Here lies Paul
He had the most beautiful feet of anyone in his time (Romans 10:15).

Here lies Timothy
There was no one else like him who took a genuine interest in the concerns of others (Philippians 2:20).

Here lies Onesiphorous
He was a truly loyal friend (2 Timothy 1:16-18).

Here lies Epaphrus
He was a great prayer warrior (Colossians 4:12).

Here lies Epenetus
He was the first convert to Christ in Asia (Romans 16:5).

Here lies Hermogenes
He dumped his friend Paul (2 Timothy 1:15).

"He dumped his friend Paul." What? That's all we know about him. When the Holy Spirit breathed out God's word, Hermogenes got written into it. If my name was going to appear in the Bible for all to review for centuries to come, I'd like the Bible to say something about me similar to what it says about Onesiphorous or Epaphrus. "Amy was a great prayer warrior" or "Amy was a truly loyal friend." I certainly wouldn't want it to say, "Amy dumped her good friend."

As Nero began persecuting Christians, and Paul went to prison for the second time, it seems likely that Hermogenes feared he might be persecuted for being friends with Paul. So he dumped Paul. Interestingly, the Holy Spirit decided Hermogenes' defection should be recorded for all posterity in Scripture. Apparently, God does not look with favor upon those who don't ever want to be hurt in relationships.

Paul may have become concerned that Timothy was tempted to become a protection-oriented friend as well. In 2 Timothy 1:8 Paul tells Timothy, "Don't be ashamed of me." Paul continues in the very next breath telling Timothy, "Join with me in suffering for the gospel."

For anyone who is a protection-oriented friend, "join with me in suffering" would be a cue to flee from the friendship. It seems many had done just that in their friendship with Paul. Phygelus, Hermogenes, and everyone in the province of Asia had already proven to be protection-oriented in their friendship with Paul. Evidence is recorded in 2 Timothy 1:15: *"You know that everyone in the province of Asia has deserted me, including Phygelus and Hermogenes."*

What would you have done if you were Paul's friend? Paul didn't exactly lead a life free of suffering.

Would you have remained Paul's friend if there was a chance you would be flogged until you were almost dead? Or would you have become a protection-oriented friend? (2 Corinthians 11:23)

Would you have remained Paul's friend if there was a chance you would be stoned and left for dead? Or would you have become a protection-oriented friend?

Would you have remained Paul's friend if there was a chance you'd be shipwrecked and left hanging onto a piece of wood in the open sea with the sharks for a day and a night?

Would you have remained Paul's friend if there was a chance you were going to be deprived of food and water?

Would you have remained Paul's friend if there was a chance you were going to be cold and naked? Or would you have become a protection-oriented friend?

Even if you had been loyal through all these hardships, at some point would you start to think, "It's time to take care of myself!"? In our "look out for number one" culture, it seems almost sinful not to be protection-oriented in such circumstances. Yet Paul writes to Timothy, "Join with me in suffering for the gospel." What advice would you give Timothy if he had asked you what to do after he got Paul's letter?

The friend who doesn't want to be hurt in relationships is easily controlled by fear. This friend may never have learned how to handle fear and so resorts to fleeing when it seems she may be hurt. Wayne and Josh Mack comment on this in their book, *Fear Factor*. They say that it's not wrong to be distressed, troubled, frightened, or to have those emotions.[18]

> Christians are not unaware of danger; they feel those natural fears, and they make wise choices while paying attention to them. God has given us this kind of natural fear for a productive purpose. It deters wickedness and prevents chaos in the world. (Christians are to be salt and light.)
>
> Fear of danger that leads one to take necessary precautions is right and holy so long as it rests upon and grows out of a faith and trust in the providence of God. The problem is, our sinful nature takes this good, helpful emotion and

---

[18] Mack, Wayne & Mack, Joshua, *The Fear Factor* (Tulsa, OK: Hensley Publishing, 2002), p. 34.

twists, perverts, and distorts it. Instead of using it for God's glory we use it for our own. As a result, it's no longer productive[19] and rather than reducing chaos it adds to it.

Heart's Desire

The protection-oriented friend closely monitors her friendships to make sure her friendships will not result in pain. She's always scared she'll be harmed. She is controlled by the desire not to be hurt.

You may become protection-oriented as a result of being badly hurt in a relationship. Perhaps the pain was a caused by:

- being abused as a child
- living through the divorce of your parents
- being dumped by a boyfriend
- being shut out of a clique
- being betrayed by a best friend who told others the secrets you told her
- being made fun of in grade school because you were overweight, had funny hair, had bad teeth, lived on the "other side of the tracks," were clumsy, or any host of other reasons.

Experiencing pain in a relationship is not a prerequisite for adopting protection as your friendship orientation. Just knowing that pain and rejection are possible and wanting to avoid suffering, may prompt you to become a protection-oriented friend. Like the aquaphobic who won't take a bath because she fears drowning, some become protection-oriented because they fear a relationship might bring pain.

For a protection-oriented friend, life is one big scary movie. Controlled by her fears, it's as if the protection-oriented friend hears the suspense music in horror films always playing in her mind. She expects the next scene in her relationships to bring pain.

Nightmare/Fear

For a friend with a protection orientation, the worst thing that could happen to her is to be hurt. Sadly, this orientation prevents the development of authentic friendships and is ineffective for a number of reasons.

---

[19] Ibid, p. 52-52.

1) To make protection your supreme goal encourages you to be self-centered. You must always be looking out for yourself. Being protection-oriented causes you to fit the description in Philippians 2:21, which says, *"For everyone looks out for his own interests, not those of Jesus Christ."*

2) Being protection-oriented causes you to develop relationships only with people whom you are confident won't hurt you. This prevents you from serving and ministering to others. Being protection-oriented causes you to focus on what you will *get* from others.

3) You are not capable of controlling others. You cannot control whether they will treat you sinfully or not. You cannot control whether they will hurt you or not.

4) Being protection-oriented causes you to pursue ephemeral, unrealistic relationships—relationships with no sin and no trials. In reality, however, two sinners make up every relationship, and any long lasting relationship will have problems and trials.

5) Being protection-oriented causes you to expect in others something you will not fulfill yourself. Because you are affected by the curse of sin there will be times when you will sin against and hurt others.

6) If you continue this way the result will be very shallow, superficial, and selfish relationships.

In the end, all the efforts of protection-oriented friends will only lead to pain. By making safe relationships their idol, they are pursuing a false god. As a result, their sorrows will increase. Psalm 16:4 states this plainly, *"The sorrows of those will increase who run after other gods…"*

Acceptable Costs

What price is the protection-oriented friend willing to pay for perceived safety? What is she willing to sacrifice? This friend is willing to end relationships when she perceives danger. She is willing to do this even if she hurts someone else in the process. This is easy to see in the case of Abram, Sarai, and Pharaoh.

Now there was a famine in the land, and Abram went down to Egypt to live there for a while because the famine was severe. As he was about to enter Egypt, he said to his wife Sarai, "I know what a beautiful woman you are. When the Egyptians see you, they will say, 'This is his wife.' Then they will kill me but will let you live. Say you are my sister, so that I will be treated well for your sake and my life will be spared because of you."

When Abram came to Egypt, the Egyptians saw that she was a very beautiful woman. And when Pharaoh's officials saw her, they praised her to Pharaoh, and she was taken into his palace. He treated Abram well for her sake, and Abram acquired sheep and cattle, male and female donkeys, menservants and maidservants, and camels.

But the LORD inflicted serious diseases on Pharaoh and his household because of Abram's wife Sarai. So Pharaoh summoned Abram. "What have you done to me?" he said. "Why didn't you tell me she was your wife? Why did you say, 'She is my sister,' so that I took her to be my wife? Now then, here is your wife. Take her and go!" Then Pharaoh gave orders about Abram to his men, and they sent him on his way, with his wife and everything he had (Genesis 12:10-20).

Put simply, Abram, concerned about what would happen to him, was protection-oriented in his new friendship with Pharaoh. Abram asked Sarai to be deceptive and to lead people to believe that she and Abram weren't married.

Can you imagine being Pharaoh? You get to know Sarai's "brother" and under your patronage Abram profits, becoming wealthy due to his friendship with you. You, however, are not prospering in this friendship. In fact, you get seriously ill, and there's no one to nurse you because everyone else is seriously ill as well. Then you find out the reason you're so sick is because you unwittingly married someone else's spouse. You might easily be tempted to be like Pharaoh, and kick Abram out of your kingdom.

If you were Abram, losing your passport and being deported from the country, what lesson do you think you should learn? Clearly, one of the lessons here is that it is very unloving to do wrong in order to try to protect yourself. In trying to protect yourself, you end up hurting others. The very thing you're trying to avoid in your life—harm—you are willing to do to others. Sadly, Abram didn't take this lesson to heart, and a few chapters later in Genesis, we see Abram again asking Sarai to tell a ruler she is his sister.

While most protection-oriented friends don't endanger the lives of others, they are willing to allow others to experience pain in order to avoid pain themselves. Protection-oriented friends care more about protecting themselves than any pain caused by ending a relationship.

The friend who doesn't want to ever be hurt is willing to accept shallow, superficial relationships out of fear that she will be hurt if anyone gets too close. Like a person wading in the shallow end of a pool, afraid to get completely wet, the protection-oriented friend won't go beyond sticking a big toe in relationships. If it seems as if the relationship will be unpleasant, she quickly jerks her big toe out of the relationship, hurries back to her beach towel, and wistfully watches others splashing and having a good time from her "safe" position on her beach towel.

Although they are unpleasant companions, the protection-oriented friend is willing to live with worry and fear. She really doesn't care for them as roommates—they insist on controlling her schedule, her phone calls, her social networking, and her outside relationships—but she's willing to put up with these companions in order to retain her protection orientation.

Ultimately this friend trusts in herself, not God. She would like to trust in others if she could be confident others wouldn't hurt her. As she tries to judge whether each person she meets is safe or unsafe, her trust is in her own judgment.

Seen in Action

The protection-oriented friend may appear shy and timid. She may turn down invitations to parties, arrive late for meetings and leave early to avoid making small talk.

Timidity is not the only method of seeking protection, however. Some protection-oriented friends seek protection by trying to gather allies. They are charming and affectionate. They may be very talkative and outgoing.

However, all of this is on their terms. They use affection, charm, and talkativeness to gain friends. Their goal is to gain allies by making sure others are favorably disposed to them.

Let's walk through a typical day of a protection-oriented friend.

6:00 am   The alarm rings and Emily shuts it off. She's already awake. In fact, she barely slept at all last night. She's been awake most of the night thinking about breaking up with Steve. Steve is starting to push for a commitment, and Emily isn't sure she's ready. To be honest, she's not sure she'll ever be ready. She's afraid of committing to a relationship with anyone.

7:30 am   Casey notices Emily getting into her car and calls, "Hi." Emily responds and then heads off to work. As Casey watches her drive away, she wonders why it's been so hard to get to know Emily. They've lived next door to each other in the same duplex for years, and yet Casey doesn't feel as if she knows Emily any better today than when she first moved in.

9:47 am   Katherine, whose office is next door to Emily's, sticks her head in to say, "Good Morning." After chatting for a few minutes Katherine heads down the hall for a meeting. Emily wonders if Katherine is after her job and is trying to see if she's doing anything wrong.

12:15 pm   Emily approaches her normal table in the cafeteria, where several of her friends are already seated. As she nears the table, the conversation dies out. Emily uncomfortably slides into a chair, sure that her friends must have been talking about her. She wonders if they've heard something about Katherine getting her job.

3:37 pm   Emily goes to her boss and volunteers to take on a new project nobody wants. Emily hopes this will make the boss her advocate if Katherine tries to take her job.

5:23 pm   Emily sits in traffic, feeling as if she is having an anxiety attack. She's been stewing about Katherine getting her job since she left work.

6:07 pm   Emily is glad she made it home without having a full blown panic attack. She wonders if she should get some help from a counselor since the attacks have been coming more frequently. Her church offers free counseling, but she's afraid to have anyone to find out that she's struggling.

7:49 pm   Emily pushes her green beans to the other side of her plate. Dinner with Steve has been very uncomfortable. She planned to break things off with him, but maybe she shouldn't. Maybe Steve won't hurt her. It sure would be nice to have a man she could trust. On the other hand, every other man she's dated hasn't been trustworthy. Could Steve really be any different? If she stays in the relationship, she's afraid she'll end up getting hurt. Maybe she should just end it now and get it over with.

9:58 pm   Emily logs into her favorite on-line chat room. She feels safe here since no one really knows her as anything other than "1776woman." "Catlover" is logged in tonight. Catlover and Emily spend the next hour chatting. Emily wishes all of her relationships could be this safe.

If you are a protection-oriented friend you probably display several of the following characteristics. Let's review these characteristics and consider what God thinks of such traits.

- <u>You are hypervigilant</u>. You are always watching for any sign hurt is coming.

  God's opinion of this: You should be vigilant to obey me. You should be vigilant to minister to others. Instead you're wasting all that energy consumed with yourself.

- <u>You are suspicious</u>. You believe others are talking about you behind your back. You believe others plan to hurt you. You don't believe the best.

  God's opinion of this: You can't know what someone is thinking unless he tells you.[20] Instead of believing the best, you are hateful.

---

[20] 1 Corinthians 2:11: For who among men knows the thoughts of a man except the man's spirit within him? In the same way no one knows the thoughts of God except the Spirit of God.

You believe the worst. You automatically assume others want to be sinful. You function as if others don't want to please God. You assume others will hurt you without caring.

- You look for someone to trust while refusing to trust anyone. You hope your next relationship will bring the safety you desire. You trust in yourself to be able to identify who is trustworthy.

  God's opinion of this: Your trust is misplaced. You trust in yourself while looking for friends you think you can trust. But mortal men will never be able to provide the protection for which you are looking (Psalm 146:3). If you would trust in Me, you wouldn't need to be controlled by fear any longer. I will never leave you nor forsake you. He who trusts in himself is a fool, but he who walks in wisdom is kept safe (Proverbs 28:26).

- You are aloof and distant. You won't be candid or open with others. You rarely divulge anything personal; divulging personal information would make you vulnerable.

  God's opinion of this: You are treating people as if they are your servants and you are their master. My Son showed friendship by being open.[21] You are just the opposite.

- You are unwilling to be vulnerable. To you, vulnerability is a curse word.

  God's opinion of this: My Son would never have died on the cross for you if He was unwilling to be vulnerable. You seem to think it was okay for Him to suffer for your sake, but you don't think you should endure any suffering.

- You run from relationships when you get scared. You end relationships with people with no explanation.

  God's opinion of this: What you despise in others, you do to them. You hate to be hurt, but you callously hurt others. You are a hypocrite.

---

[21] John 15:15: I no longer call you servants, because a servant does not know his master's business. Instead, I have called you friends, for everything that I learned from my Father I have made known to you.

- <u>You try to make others like you</u>. You sometimes try to defend yourself by trying to make others favorably disposed toward you. You may be charming and engaging.

  God's opinion of this: You are trying to use people to gain their goodwill and their protection. I want you to love and serve others, not use others.

- <u>You sometimes chatter incessantly</u>. You use constant talking as a defense to prevent anyone from asking you questions. You control the conversation.

  God's opinion of this: When words are many sin is not absent. You are sinning by using your speech to control others. You ought to be using your speech to edify and build up others.

- <u>You don't want anyone to know your weaknesses</u>. You want everyone to think you are strong.

  God's opinion of this: By trying to hide your weaknesses you hide my power. My power is made perfect in weakness.

What Others Experience

<u>Your initial experience may be positive</u>.

You may initially be drawn to a protection-oriented friend. She may appear fragile and elicit your compassion, or she may appear charming and seem to be very open to friendship.

Control-oriented friends may easily connect with protection-oriented friends. Control-oriented friends may perceive they can gain control by offering protection. Because they seem to be able to manage everybody and everything, the protection-oriented friend may believe a control-oriented friend can keep her safe.

<u>You feel shut out</u>.

You may feel as if you are being kept at arm's length in your friendship with a protection-oriented friend. Although you invest energy and put effort into the friendship, it may seem as if you can never really get to know this friend. Like someone in the witness protection program whose background has been sanitized and who now lives a new identity, the protection-oriented friend carefully guards against letting you beyond the barriers she has erected.

Your relationships end with no explanation.

When you develop a friendship with a protection-oriented friend, you may find that the relationship suddenly grows cold. Your friend may not attend activities if she knows you'll be there, she may not return phone calls, and she may drop out of ministry commitments.

You are puzzled about what happened. You thought you had built a relationship with this friend, only to find you've been abandoned like a house whose owners default on their mortgage. Like neighbors who wake up to an empty home next door, you find your friendship has dematerialized. You are left hurt and confused. You accepted the protection-oriented friend and let her into your life only to be dumped.

You may try to become her protector.

You may be tempted to try to become the protector of your protection-oriented friend. In order to encourage your friend to feel safe in the friendship, you may promise that you won't hurt your friend. However, there is a problem with this. What your protection-oriented friend really needs is to trust in God, not you.

Because of the curse of sin, it's highly likely that at some point you will make a sinful choice that will directly or indirectly lead your protection-oriented friend to believe you are not trustworthy. Perhaps you have a bad habit of running late, or not returning phone calls, or over-committing and having to cancel plans. Any one of those sins, or a host of others, can cause a protection-oriented friend to determine you are not trustworthy. (And this simply reinforces her reasoning that she needs to be protection-oriented. See, another friend has been untrustworthy!)

What your protection-oriented friend needs is to trust in God. Then she can face even the most painful relationship with confidence because she knows that God will work it for her good, to help her become more like Christ.

<u>You may become protection-oriented in your friendships</u>.

Friendship with a protection-oriented friend may be a snare for you. As a result of your friendship, you may be tempted to become protection-oriented also. Remember that Paul may have been concerned that Timothy would follow the example of Hermogenes, Phygelus and all Asia in deserting him. Friendship with someone whose first priority is self-preservation may spread like the swine flu to you, with the same unwelcome effects.

Just as coming in contact with a flu victim increases the probability the virus will spread to you, contact with a protection-oriented friend increases the probability that you will be tempted to adopt her philosophy of self-preservation. Just as an open wound gives easy access to germs from a virus, the wounds you receive when you are held at arm's length or dumped by your protection-oriented friend, make it easy to be infected with a protection orientation.

In the end, rather than knowing the joy of loving God and loving others, the protection-oriented friend lives in a barren wasteland, ruled by only trusting and loving herself.

Chapter 7
The Rightness-Oriented Friend
Friends Who are Concerned About Being Proper

With her witty and pithy replies, Miss Manners has come to be an accepted authority on matters of etiquette. Asked to settle disputes on matters ranging from answering the phone, whose names should be printed in an obituary notice, serving appetizers before dinner, how to address your doctor, and the definition of casual dress, Miss Manners advice column is carried by scores of newspapers. Those who want to know what is "right" correspond with Miss Manners to get her judgment on how they or others should conduct themselves.

Suppose you were Miss Manners and received the following letter. How would you answer?

Dear Miss Manners:
As teachers at our school, we are required to sit with our students during their lunch period. At a recent event, the students from one classroom failed to wash their hands properly before eating. When I pointed out their failure to the teacher, he didn't do anything about it. Shouldn't he have required his students to wash their hands properly?

We'll never know how Miss Manners would have replied to this letter. However, we are able to see the response of an even more qualified authority on what is right and best. We find God's answer to this question in Mark 7:1-23:

> *The Pharisees and some of the teachers of the law who had come from Jerusalem gathered around Jesus and saw some of his disciples eating food with hands that were "unclean," that is, unwashed. (The Pharisees and all the Jews do not eat unless they give their hands a ceremonial washing, holding to the tradition of the elders. When they come from the marketplace they do not eat unless they wash. And they observe many other traditions, such as the washing of cups, pitchers and kettles.)*
>
> *So the Pharisees and teachers of the law asked Jesus, "Why don't your disciples live according to the tradition of the elders instead of eating their food with 'unclean' hands?"*
>
> *He replied, "... You have let go of the commands of God and are holding on to the traditions of men.*
>
> *"Don't you see that nothing that enters a man from the outside can make him 'unclean'? For it doesn't go into his heart but into his stomach, and then out of his body."...*
>
> *He went on: "What comes out of a man is what makes him 'unclean.' For from within, out of men's hearts, come evil thoughts, sexual immorality, theft, murder, adultery, greed, malice, deceit, lewdness, envy, slander, arrogance and folly. All these evils come from inside and make a man 'unclean.'"*

Pithier than a response from Miss Manners, God, the Ultimate Authority on rightness made the point that what is important is the heart.

Heart's Desire

Like the Pharisees described above, the rightness-oriented friend thinks others should do things the way she believes is right. She is very concerned about being proper.

In effect, because she is convinced that her way is right, the rightness-oriented friend functions as if she is the final standard for what is right and wrong. Everyone ought to do things her way because her way is the "right" way. She becomes the judge, ignoring God's warning in James 4:11-12[22] not to promote oneself to that position.

The friend who is concerned about being proper doesn't want to be bothered by people who do things wrong. In her mind, there is a right way to do things, and she wants everyone around her to follow the rules. Although it may superficially appear that the standard for her "rules" is Scripture, a closer look reveals that her standard is really herself. The Bible is simply a tool to lend authority to her desires.

In an earlier chapter, we saw that a control-oriented friend also wants her friends to do things her way. The rightness-oriented friend differs from a control-oriented friend in that she is not overly concerned about having power over others. She is more likely to write off those who don't do right, while a control-oriented friend will vigorously strive to get the upper hand.

The friend who is concerned about being proper also has similarities to the prestige-oriented friend we will meet in an upcoming chapter. However, while the prestige-oriented friend may actively desire to be put on a pedestal, the rightness-oriented friend doesn't necessarily yearn for this. Her goal is not so much to have others look up to her as it is to have others do what she thinks is correct. She is not averse to having others put her on a pedestal, but she's not actively striving for exalted status. She will simply take it as a matter of course that others think well of her. After all, why shouldn't they? She is doing what is right.

The friend who is concerned about being proper is not overly troubled by the thought of being disliked. The only plausible reason for anyone to dislike her is because that person doesn't want to do right. Since the rightness-oriented friend spurns those who don't want to do right, she is not concerned about their opinion. She might even boast about how a person intent on doing wrong was not happy with her.

The rightness-oriented friend generally accepts as friends those who meet her standards of rightness. In fact, she probably won't be friends

---

[22] James 4:11-12: Brothers, do not slander one another. Anyone who speaks against his brother or judges him speaks against the law and judges it. When you judge the law, you are not keeping it, but sitting in judgment on it. There is only one Lawgiver and Judge, the one who is able to save and destroy. But you—who are you to judge your neighbor?

with wrong doers, citing as support Scripture that warns against bad companions. While Scripture certainly does warn about the dangers of bad companions, the rightness-oriented friend tends to minimize any verses about being salt and light in a corrupt world and maximize verses about avoiding bad companions. She is unbalanced in her application of these verses. She isn't concerned she will be tempted to do wrong, she just doesn't want to put up with those who don't do right.

In what may seem totally out of character, sometimes you may observe the rightness-oriented friend working with the lowest echelons of society. However, she will see herself as a savior doing good work among undeserving people. She considers herself to be in a class separate from those whom she is serving. She doesn't know that she is just like them. She does not see herself as someone with a desperately wicked heart. She doesn't see herself as someone who daily needs the grace of our Savior. The rightness-oriented friend sees herself as superior and her patience runs out quickly if those with whom she works don't change rapidly.

Nightmare/Fear

Those who make social blunders, don't follow prescribed social practices, or are socially inept are all would-be nightmares for the friend who is concerned about being proper. Like Simon the Pharisee in Luke 7:36ff, the rightness-oriented friend would be horrified if a prostitute poured perfume over Christ's feet and wiped His feet with her hair while Christ was dining at her home. Such behavior is not correct or decorous. Christ should not have any association with a prostitute, and He certainly shouldn't allow her to touch Him like that!

The rightness-oriented friend assumes that others will think negatively of her if her friends are not polished and socially correct. She fears that others would attribute the characteristics of any unpolished friends to her. As a result, she carefully judges and critiques the mannerisms, behaviors, and speech of those with whom she associates.

The rightness-oriented friend does not want to have to put up with people who won't follow the rules. Nor does she want to be associated with people who don't take the rules seriously. She dislikes people who don't follow socially acceptable behavior and is peeved when others ignorantly violate what she considers proper etiquette.

Acceptable Cost

The friend who is concerned about being proper is willing to make several sacrifices to maintain her friendship orientation. One of the costs associated with this orientation is being self-deceived about the nature of her heart. It's entirely likely the rightness-oriented friend has deluded herself and sincerely believes she is a good—perhaps superior—person. However, 1 John makes it clear that if we claim to have no sin, we deceive ourselves.

In her friendships, this person never asks to be held accountable for growth in any significant areas. Although her friends may confess that they are struggling with fear, anger, worry, or jealousy; these sins don't seem to be present in her life. The rightness-oriented friend sees herself as different from others—while they may struggle with sin in a major way; her struggles are more like minor skirmishes. She sees herself as a basically good person. She is very willing to pray that her less mature friends will overcome their struggles and perhaps is secretly glad that she's not like them.

The rightness-oriented friend is deceived by a belief that it's acceptable for her to be the judge and that her judgments are correct. She doesn't realize there is only one lawgiver and judge—the one who is able to save and destroy.

The friend who is concerned about being proper is willing to function as a self-righteous Pharisee.

- Like the Pharisees, she is quick to notice when someone does something she believes is wrong (Mark 7:1-23).

- Like the Pharisees, she sets herself as the standard and feels free to judge others (Matthew 12:2; John 7:48).

- Like the Pharisees, she cares little about where people will spend eternity (Matthew 23:13) but cares a lot about nitpicky things (Matthew 23:23).

- Like the Pharisees, she wants others to conform to her standards (Matthew 23:15).

- Like the Pharisees, she finds self-righteousness acceptable.

The rightness-oriented friend is satisfied with standards that are based solely on externals. As long as she and her friends look good on the outside, she is not troubled that her heart may be corrupt. This is tragic because God uses a different standard. God announces His standard in Jeremiah 17:10. *"I the LORD search the heart and examine the mind, to reward a man according to his conduct, according to what his deeds deserve."*

At the judgment seat, many will be told *"Depart from me, I never knew you"* (Matthew 25:41). When they protest and point out how good they looked on the outside—we did all these good things—the verdict won't change. Tragically, this may be the price some with a rightness orientation will be required to pay. Some may learn too late that they never really knew Christ.

Seen in Action

Let's walk through a typical day with a rightness-oriented friend.

7:00 am   Justine finishes breakfast and carries her cereal bowl to the sink. She sees that her sister has left her rinsed cereal bowl in the sink again. Justine has asked her sister several times to put her bowl in the dishwasher rather than leave it in the sink. In the past Justine has patiently explained that she and her sister should live as though guests would be welcome in their home at any time. That means keeping the apartment picked up, the bathroom sinks free of hair and toothpaste, and the kitchen counters wiped clean with dishes deposited in the dishwasher. Justine's sister has irreverently responded that she likes living in a clean apartment too, but she thinks its fine to simply rinse her dishes off and leave them in the sink. Giving her best martyr sigh, Justine puts both her bowl and her sister's bowl in the dishwasher.

7:40 am   As Justine pulls out of her parking space in their apartment lot, she notices that Ryan, their friendly next door neighbor, has parked in Mrs. Tuttle's space again. Justine doesn't understand why Ryan doesn't park in his own space. She knows Mrs. Tuttle has stopped driving and doesn't care if Ryan parks in her spot, but the apartment handbook says residents are to park in their own spaces.

8:10 am   As one of the city's most respected interior designers, Justine has a number of wealthy clients. Her first client this morning is Elaine Basingstoke, an old college sorority sister. Elaine wants to redo her master bedroom and has already had a preliminary meeting with Justine to go over her preferences.

Justine instructs her design assistant to set up easels for the design boards she'll need for her pitch to Elaine. This pitch must be handled adroitly since Justine has chosen a different color scheme than the one Elaine indicated was her preference. Justine is sure that she can convince her sorority sister that the colors Elaine has chosen just aren't right. Justine has put together her design boards using the colors she believes will work much better in the master bedroom.

9:25 am   Justine accepts a phone call from Chris Connolly. Chris and Justine went to school together and even double dated a couple times. Several years ago, Chris pointed out an engineering flaw in one of Justine's designs for the Center for Performing Arts. While Justine has been civil to him since that time, she has never forgiven him for making her look bad in front of the entire city council.

11:33 am   Elaine leaves Justine's office with a bit of a bad taste in her mouth. Justine is probably right about the color scheme, but it seems to Elaine that since it's her home, her designer should try to follow her preferences. Justine seems to act like Elaine is too ignorant to know what she will like best in her bedroom. Elaine knows Justine's design will look great, but she wonders if she should find a designer who isn't such a prima donna, one who respects the customer's preferences.

12:00 pm   Justine grabs a folder off her desk to take to her lunch with Taylor. Yesterday on the phone Taylor was sure Union Street was a one-way street going south and Clairmont ran parallel going north. Justine was sure Union was one-way going north and Clairmont went south. Justine has printed off a map to prove to Taylor that she was right.

3:15 pm   Justine responds to an e-mail from her friend Katrina that St. Anthony's hospital has just received a $35 million grant for a new addition. Katrina has worked on this grant for months and faced a lot of stiff competition. Justine sends a nice reply and follows up by sending flowers because that seems like the right thing to do.

6:28 pm   Justine hurriedly finishes filling in the answers in the discussion guide her small group Bible study is using. The group meets in half an hour, and Justine hasn't opened the book or the study guide since she laid them on her desk after the last small group meeting.

7:06 pm   Justine grabs a seat next to April at Jason and Diane's house, as everyone gets ready for their small group discussion to begin. She notices disapprovingly that April doesn't have her study guide completely filled in.

9:00 pm   Jason, who is leading the study, announces it is time for prayer requests. Justine jots down the following requests:

            Diane: Put off laziness in regard to housework. She has been choosing to watch TV all evening rather than keep up with her responsibilities for the house.

            Charlie: Show honor to his parents. Charlie explains that he was rebellious growing up and developed habits of speaking to his parents with a disrespectful tone. Someone recently pointed out that when he speaks to his parents on the phone he is terse and impatient with them. Charlie wants to grow in genuinely honoring his parents.

            Jason: Wants to work heartily and respectfully for his employer. This is tough right now, because he doesn't agree with some of the decisions his boss has made.

            April: Wants to put off sinful worry. A single mom, April has been worrying about her kids when they go out with their friends, fearing they will be in an accident. She has found herself calling them repeatedly to make sure they are okay.

When it's Justine's turn, she asks the group to pray that she'll be able to get everything done that she needs to accomplish. She explains that she's very busy at work right now, and has taken on several big projects.

9:25 pm   Justine thanks Jason for leading the Bible study. She tells Jason she thinks he's a great teacher.

9:30 pm   April leaves the small group wishing she could be like Justine. Justine always seems to have her act together and doesn't seem to struggle with problems as April does.

9:48 pm   Justine's sister is curled up on the sofa reading when Justine returns from Bible study. An empty teacup sits on the end table next to her. Justine hopes her sister remembers to pick it up before she goes to bed. When Misty asks how small group was Justine replies that it was fine. She adds, "Jason could do a better job of leading. Twice tonight he couldn't think of the reference for the verse he mentioned when he answered questions from the group."

Justine plops her Bible, book, and study guide on her desk and heads for bed.

If you are a friend who is concerned about being proper, you probably display several of the following characteristics. Let's review these characteristics and see what God thinks of these traits.

* <u>You want everyone around you to do what is right in your eyes</u>. You want a nice, tidy world so that you won't be bothered. In your world, everyone should be punctual, neat, and well-mannered.

  God's opinion of this: You are concerned about everyone else doing right, yet you yourself are breaking the royal law (James 2:8). You do not love your neighbor; you're simply using the law to condemn your neighbor. You're very concerned about everyone following the rules, but you don't really care about people. You love rules, not people. You don't seem to realize that the law is only a tool to lead us to Christ. There's something better than rules and the law—being justified by faith in my perfect Son (Galatians 3:24)!

Your concern with rightness will result in repeated disappointment and frustration because the law can't make anything perfect (as you desire) (Hebrews 7:19). However, you can have a better hope—you can draw near to Me through Jesus Christ (Hebrews 7:19). Christ is perfect! He should be your hope.

- <u>You are very aware of others' wrongs</u>. You mentally take note of any infraction committed by others. You notice when others park in the wrong space, when others don't use the correct grammar, when others have a typo in their PowerPoint presentation, and so on.

  God's opinion of this: Do you really want to be judged the way you judge others? After you've invested hours in putting together a presentation, do you want the only feedback you get to be about the typo on page 5? When you've worked hard to change a sinful habit, do you want others just to focus on what you're still doing wrong? When you're trying to convey an important point, do you want others to remember you used the wrong verb tense? In the same way you judge others, you will be judged, and with the measure you use, it will be measured to you (Matthew 7:2).

- <u>You rarely extend grace and mercy when others experience difficulties</u>. You tend to believe others have gotten what they deserve and that we shouldn't interfere with the Lord's discipline. In your opinion, those who experience consequences because they are guilty should learn from their consequences, not have their burden lightened.

  God's opinion of this: You are like the unmerciful servant in Matthew 18. He callously disregarded the fact that he had been forgiven a huge debt and unmercifully demanded payment of a smaller debt from a debtor.

- <u>You establish standards which you believe everyone should follow</u>. Others should keep the house clean according to your specifications, wear their clothes as you think proper, and follow your rules of correct behavior. You are scrupulous and punctilious.

God's opinion of this: You put heavy loads on people just like the Pharisees (Matthew 23:4). Don't you realize that your righteous acts are rubbish (Isaiah 64:6; Philippians 3:8)?

- <u>You view yourself as a martyr when others don't live up to your standards</u>. In your self-talk you ask, "Why am I the only one that seems to care about doing things right?"

God's opinion of this: You are concerned about rightness, but you've made rules an end in themselves, not a tool to lead people to Me. Therefore, it's no wonder you feel sorry for yourself. Your focus isn't on Me, it's on you. You are like Martha who was so concerned about preparing food that she missed the big picture (Luke 10:38-42). She was missing an opportunity to learn from my Son, the perfect representation of what is right.

- <u>You are easily annoyed when others don't do things the way you think they ought to be done or when they don't follow the rules</u>. You fume about neighbors who don't obey the covenants of the neighborhood association; you fume about colleagues who don't answer your e-mails quickly enough; and you fume about extended family members who don't let you know if they'll be able to come for the holidays at least a month in advance.

God's opinion of this: You fume about all these things without recognizing that you are demonstrating sinful anger, and you are not being loving (love is not easily angered). Although you're familiar with Proverbs 12:16 that a fool shows her annoyance at once, you don't realize you're the fool.

- <u>You get angry and hold grudges if someone makes you look bad in the eyes of others</u>. You have a mental list of folks who have made you look bad. You keep the list updated and current. Once someone is put on the list, it's almost impossible to be removed from it.

God's opinion of this: If you look bad because you've done something wrong, the correct response is to humbly admit it, not get sinfully angry. Your response is motivated by pride. I hate pride!

- <u>You are condescending</u>. You appear gracious in public, but you are often critical in private.

  God's opinion of this: You are a hypocrite. Your nice words are just like the kisses of an enemy (Proverbs 27:6).

- <u>You appear to have it all together</u>. To others, you don't appear to struggle with sin. Your prayer requests tend to show off your strengths more than plead for help with sinful habits. You enjoy having others believe you have it together.

  God's opinion of this: All righteous works are as filthy rags. What you put on display is in reality a heap of garbage. It's pathetic that you would point to a heap of stinking garbage with pride.

- <u>You almost never ask forgiveness</u>. Since you believe you're practically perfect and don't mess up, you never see the need to ask forgiveness.

  God's opinion of this: You are deluded and self-deceived. You have made Me out to be a liar, and my word has no place in your life (1 John 1:8, 10).

What Others Experience

<u>Your initial experience may be enjoyable.</u>

It's fun to have friends that seem to have it all together. You're never embarrassed by them. They seem to handle life well. They seem to be successful. Friendship with a friend who is concerned about being proper may initially be very attractive.

Prestige-oriented friends may find it especially easy to connect with rightness-oriented friends. Because the heart's desire of the prestige-oriented friend is to be well regarded, friendship with someone who is focused on doing what's proper may seem to be advantageous.

<u>You feel like you are not able to measure up.</u>

The rightness-oriented friend seems to have it all together. She never talks about personal battles with sin. Like Mary Poppins who declares that she is practically perfect in every way, the rightness-oriented friend seems to lead a life that from all appearances is practically perfect. You, on the other hand, know that there are many areas in your life where you need to change and grow. Hard as you try, you don't see that you could ever be on an equal plane with someone who seems to have it all together.

<u>You aren't shown mercy</u>.

When you mess up, your rightness-oriented friend is unlikely to treat you compassionately, or with grace and mercy. If you experience painful consequences as a result of your failure, don't be surprised if her attitude is, "You got what you deserved."

When you offend your rightness-oriented friend, you have to demonstrate extreme submission or repentance in order to be forgiven. Forgiveness is granted grudgingly, and you walk away feeling like your friend is upset and that you owe her something. Forgiveness does not result in a sweeter relationship.

<u>You are often corrected, even if what you are doing is not sinful</u>.

A friend who will come alongside you to help you escape from the snares of sin is a friend to be treasured. Such a friend will lovingly confront you about areas in your life in which you are displeasing God, and patiently encourage and love you as you battle to change sinful habits. The rightness-oriented friend will confront you, but she uses her preferences, desires, and rules as the standard for her correction, not love for you and a desire to see you have sweet fellowship with our Lord. Consequently, her correction is often unhelpful and unloving.

<u>You see your friend as superior</u>.

You may be tempted to put your rightness-oriented friend on a pedestal and treat her as if she is superior to others.

<u>You may begin striving to look good on the outside, caring little about the inside</u>.

You may be tempted to follow the example of your friend who is concerned about being proper and become just as concerned as she is about looking good on the outside. Like the Pharisees whom Jesus rebuked for whitewashing the outside of a tomb when the inside was full of maggots, you try to appear pristine on the outside, content to live with a heart that is corrupt. Additionally, you may begin to believe you shouldn't be genuine and open about your struggles in life.

Those who understand what God says about the sinful nature will at some point realize that their friendship with a rightness-oriented person isn't genuine. God describes our hearts as desperately wicked, not oozing with rightness or goodness. At some point, you will begin to see that a friendship with someone who never fails is superficial. Your friendship is not genuine and authentic.

Chapter 8

The Pleasure-Oriented Friend
Friends Who Just Want to Have Fun

Heart's Desire

The heart of the pleasure-oriented friend is controlled by the craving for fun. This friend is ruled by her desire for what brings her happiness or gives her a buzz. She seeks personal gratification. She wants to be entertained. Like those in Romans 1:25, she seeks for pleasure in the creation, not the Creator.

Acceptable Cost

"Get her for me!"

"But son," said the Jewish father, "can't you find a nice Jewish girl to marry? How can you marry someone from those uncircumcised heathens? Surely we can find a wife for you among our people. What about …?"

"Get her for me. She's the right one for me," replied his intransigent son.[23] Or as the NASB puts it, *"She looks good to me."*

---

[23] Judges 14:2-3, paraphrase

And so, the very first time we see Samson as an adult, he's pursuing his pleasure. Samson proclaims, "Get her for me; she's the one for me."

Samson is the Old Testament party boy. Although set apart by God as a judge for Israel, Samson didn't take this job seriously. It seems that Samson was too busy chasing women. The acceptable cost of Samson's pleasure orientation was ignoring God's design for his life. Called by God before his birth to be a judge of Israel, Samson was better suited to be judged, than to judge.

We know how Samson hooked up with Delilah, but Delilah is only one of the women Samson pursued. Scripture first records that Samson told his parents he intended to marry a Philistine girl he saw. (That didn't work out so well, by the way.) Later Scripture records that Samson saw a prostitute and went after her. The last in Samson's succession of women was Delilah.

As we know, Delilah was in cahoots with the Philistine rulers to learn the secret of Samson's strength. The party boy's affair with Delilah ended as the Philistines successfully overcame him, gouged out his eyes, and tossed him in prison. The cost of being pleasure-oriented was *and is* high.

Was Samson unaware of God's requirements? Was Samson never taught that God is a holy God who cannot look upon sin with favor? Did no one ever explain to Samson that if you love God and follow His commands you will be blessed, but if you turn away from Him and are disobedient you will be destroyed (Deuteronomy 30)? Was Samson unaware that you reap what you sow? Did no one teach Samson to delight in God?

Is Samson's story just some antiquated memoir with no relevance to our time? How does a man being captured by the Philistines and having his eyes gouged out apply to being a pleasure-oriented friend?

Did Samson plan to have his eyes gouged out? Did he think, "I know I'll end up a slave, but Delilah is worth it?" Samson didn't really believe he would experience negative consequences for pursuing his pleasure orientation. Likewise, pleasure-oriented friends today don't expect to experience any consequences for living to have fun.

"She's the one for me." Today Samson could have said, "I'm in love." And what prompted him to fall in love? He saw her, and she looked good to him. He thought she would make him happy.

Are we really that much different from Samson? When we sit in a restaurant with our friends and notice the looks of the men around us, and comment, "He's so hot," aren't we basically saying, "He looks good to me." When we speculate what it might be like to "hook up" with that guy who is really hot, how much different are we from Samson seeing a prostitute and going to bed with her? Do the scruples that hold us back from buying sex make us somehow more pure? Not from Christ's standpoint. *"Whoever looks at a woman lustfully has already committed adultery with her in his heart"* (Matthew 5:28). Perhaps that could be paraphrased, "Whoever examines the physiques of the men around her, has already hooked up with them in her heart."

Pleasure-oriented friends pursue what looks good to them. Maybe it's sex; maybe it's not sex. Maybe it's food, or wine, or music, or entertainment, or possessions, or being a dare devil, or work. Pleasure-oriented friends pursue what they believe will give them pleasure.

Pleasure-oriented friends are generally happy to be friends with anyone who will join them in their pursuit of pleasure. Conversely, those who hinder them in their pursuit of pleasure are likely to experience their wrath. In Samson's case, those who hindered him in his pursuit of pleasure often ended up dead. While most pleasure-oriented friends don't physically commit murder, many with this orientation use their tongue as a weapon, leaving wounded behind.

Acceptable Cost

The pleasure-oriented friend is willing to sacrifice self-discipline and self-control. The hard work sometimes required in relationships interferes with pleasure, and rather than invest the effort, it is easier to let problems remain unsolved, and let others do the hard work. Although she may invest effort and labor into things that bring her pleasure, such effort will seem too costly if there is no immediate pleasure payoff. Instead, she will do what is immediately fun. Pleasure-oriented friends are willing to give up genuine joy in order to have short term pleasure. Sadly, the pleasure they desire is not the satisfaction of pleasing God. The delight of pleasing God is sacrificed for whatever will bring an immediate rush. Feelings trump godliness.

Those who are pleasure-oriented are willing to abandon commitments if something better comes along. Similarly, they may avoid making commitments in order to keep their options open. If you ask your pleasure-oriented friend to come over for dinner she may want to know who else is coming. If she is satisfied that your other guests will not be boring, she may commit to attend. Although she made the commitment, you may wait in vain for the doorbell to announce her arrival if she is invited to do something more appealing.

Using destructive speech is another acceptable cost for the pleasure-oriented friend. In some cases this may be complaining, in some it may be brutal personal attacks. Unlike the approval-oriented friend, the pleasure-oriented friend is not overly concerned whether you like her or not. If you get in the way of her pleasure, she is likely to display sinful anger. Like Samson, who set the fields of his killjoy friends on fire, the pleasure-oriented friend will use her tongue as a fire.

Nightmare/Fear

The pleasure-oriented friend's nightmare is being bored, being stuck with people who are serious (who aren't oriented around the next fun activity), or being forced to sacrifice pleasure. She takes little joy in faithfulness. Repetition and perseverance become boring, and God's delight in faithfulness holds no motivation. God's promise of reward to the faithful is disregarded. A crown of life in the future can't compete with pleasure at this moment.

The pleasure-oriented friend often makes it clear that she's not interested in being serious or being around those who are. She may have learned to be the life of the party, the one everyone looks to for the next fun event. Getting stuck with someone who is serious is no fun. It's agony. "Lighten up, don't take things so seriously" may be her injunction to anyone who seems to endanger her pursuit of fun.

Because she has never learned the joy of pleasing God, the pleasure-oriented friend doesn't want to sacrifice pleasure. What would she live for? Life would be meaningless. She would be living a nightmare. She doesn't understand that the path she is on is a superhighway leading to meaninglessness. People lots smarter than she (in fact, the wisest man ever to live before Christ) have tried to live for pleasure and ended up determining life isn't worth living—life is meaningless.

Seen in Action

Let's walk through a typical day of a pleasure-oriented friend, looking at how her orientation is seen in action.

10:30 am   Aroused from sleep as her cell phone blares "Girls Just Want to Have Fun," Ellie gropes for her phone to see who's calling. The caller ID registers that it's Jacob, and Ellie groggily mumbles, "Hello."

"Hey, are you up yet?" is Jacob's friendly greeting.

"Why would you think I was up? I was out dancing with you last night until 2 am."

"You can get your beauty sleep some other time," Jacob responds. "Paul's girlfriend is in town and a bunch of us are headed to IHOP for brunch at 11. If you don't get moving, you're going to miss it."

11:20 am   Ellie arrives at IHOP, slides into a seat next to Maria, and orders French toast.

For the next hour and a half, Ellie and her friends trade gossip and sarcastic put- downs. Things break up when Ellie and Maria decide to go to the mall.

1:45 pm   "That looks really cute on you. You should get that," Ellie urges Maria.

"I don't know," Maria debates. "I promised myself I was going to quit using my credit card."

"It's only $20. You should get it," Ellie urges.

2:13 pm   "Girls Just Want to Have Fun" blares from Ellie's purse again. This time it's Jeanie. Clearly heartbroken, Jeanie tearfully tells Ellie that she and Bryce broke up last night.

"Oh Jeanie, I'm so sorry. He was no fun anyway. Now you can go out with us tonight. I'll introduce you to Jacob's cousin. He is really handsome."

2:35 pm   Maria comes out of the dressing room as Ellie is punching in Bryce's cell phone number. When Bryce picks up, Ellie launches into him.

"How could you do that to Jeanie? You think you're too good for her or what?" Barely giving Bryce a chance to reply, Ellie continues, "So what was it? You just wanted out? You found someone else?"

When Bryce responds that he thinks what happened should be between him and Jeanie, Ellie erupts in rage. "So why won't you tell me the truth? You're just a lying two-timer who thinks he's too good for Jeanie. Well, you know what; you could never be good enough for her in a million years."

As Ellie's voice gets louder and louder, Maria grabs her arm and drags her out of the mall.

3:15 pm   Ellie spends two hours on Facebook, slamming Bryce for dumping Jeanie.

5:25 pm   Macy calls and invites Ellie to a women's retreat hosted by their church. "How boring," thinks Ellie and gets off the phone as quickly as possible.

7:30 pm   Ellie waits in the crowded foyer of the Cheesecake Factory with a big group of her friends. Jeanie has come and the girls are scoping out guys, trying to find someone who looks good for Jeanie.

9:25 pm   The group leaves the Cheesecake Factory and heads for a new coffee house which has live entertainment. The new coffee house is fun, and they stay until it closes.

12:30 am   Ellie and her friends stand in front of the coffee house and figure out which restaurants are open all night. They ridicule Regina when she decides to go home and go to bed. After she's gone, they start gossiping about Mike, the new guy Regina has been seeing. They place bets on whether Regina's going home to bed or whether she's going to spend the night at Mike's house.

3:15 am   Ellie falls into bed, making sure to turn off her phone and alarm. She's glad tomorrow is Sunday so that she can sleep 'til noon.

Perhaps you have friends like Ellie. Perhaps you *are* Ellie. Let's consider what God might say to the Ellie's of this world when He observes the characteristics often found in pleasure-oriented friends.

* <u>Your friendships are all about having fun</u>. Your purpose in having friends and spending time with them is solely to have fun. Friendship is all about pleasure—hanging out together, going shopping, and eating out. It's never about serving together, stretching each other spiritually, or helping each other grow. It's never about ministry or holding each other accountable.

  God's opinion of this: Your life is vain. It is going nowhere. In the end you will find you have wasted your life.[24]

* <u>You gossip</u>. Talking about people is just another way to have fun. To you, sharing nuggets of juicy information simply adds spice to your conversation.

  God's opinion of this: You destroy friendships with your gossip. I would advise people to avoid you.[25]

* <u>You offer shallow comfort to those who are hurting</u>. Because you've oriented your life around pleasure, you don't have anything substantial to offer to those who are suffering. The best you can do is try to temporarily cheer them up.

  God's opinion of this: You don't have the depth of character to really comfort someone who is hurting. Your comfort actually ends up

---

[24] When Solomon lived for pleasure, he concluded life wasn't worth living. Ecclesiastes 2:10-11: I denied myself nothing my eyes desired; I refused my heart no pleasure. My heart took delight in all my work, and this was the reward for all my labor. Yet when I surveyed all that my hands had done and what I had toiled to achieve, everything was meaningless, a chasing after the wind; nothing was gained under the sun.

[25] Proverbs 16:28: A perverse man stirs up dissension, and a gossip separates close friends. Proverbs 20:19: A gossip betrays a confidence; so avoid a man who talks too much.

causing more pain, just like someone who takes away a coat on a cold day.[26]

• <u>You are a mocker</u>. You deride people who don't meet with your approval. What you call teasing is often thinly disguised ridicule of those you don't like.

God's opinion of this: As you laugh at others, you show contempt for me. Since you have loved mockery, prepare for wisdom to mock you. It won't be pretty.[27]

• <u>You try to get others to embrace your idol</u>. You accuse others of being too straight-laced, serious, or stodgy. You ask, "What's wrong with having fun? Loosen up. One time won't kill you."

God's opinion of this: When you encourage your friends to take small steps toward a pleasure-oriented life, reasoning that a little won't harm them, whether you realize it or not, you are leading them toward sin. Desire and sin don't start out full-grown.[28] You are just like Folly who entices the simple saying, "Come in here."[29] You

---

[26] Proverbs 25:20: Like one who takes away a garment on a cold day, or like vinegar poured on soda, is one who sings songs to a heavy heart.

[27] Proverbs 1:20-33: Wisdom calls aloud in the street, she raises her voice in the public squares; at the head of the noisy streets she cries out, in the gateways of the city she makes her speech: "How long will you simple ones love your simple ways? How long will mockers delight in mockery and fools hate knowledge? If you had responded to my rebuke, I would have poured out my heart to you and made my thoughts known to you. But since you rejected me when I called and no one gave heed when I stretched out my hand, since you ignored all my advice and would not accept my rebuke, I in turn will laugh at your disaster; I will mock when calamity overtakes you— when calamity overtakes you like a storm, when disaster sweeps over you like a whirlwind, when distress and trouble overwhelm you. "Then they will call to me but I will not answer; they will look for me but will not find me. Since they hated knowledge and did not choose to fear the LORD, since they would not accept my advice and spurned my rebuke, they will eat the fruit of their ways and be filled with the fruit of their schemes. For the waywardness of the simple will kill them, and the complacency of fools will destroy them; but whoever listens to me will live in safety and be at ease, without fear of harm."

[28] Don't be deceived. Sin doesn't begin full blown. James 1:14-15: Each one is tempted when, by his own evil desire, he is dragged away and enticed. Then, after desire has conceived, it gives birth to sin; and sin, when it is full-grown, gives birth to death.

[29] Proverbs 9:13-16: The woman Folly is loud; she is undisciplined and without knowledge. She sits at the door of her house, on a seat at the highest point of the city,

are not a good friend to have; you are a bad friend, because bad companions corrupt good character.[30]

• <u>You focus on externals</u>. You emphasize looks and minimize character, because our culture promotes the idea that pleasure is associated with beauty.

  God's opinion of this: I look at the heart. Emphasizing looks will encourage you to develop close friendships with those I would reject.[31]

• <u>You are opinionated</u>. You delight in giving your opinion on everything from restaurants to boyfriends, from hair color to the best ice cream.

  God's opinion of this: You delight in the same thing a fool delights in, airing your own opinion.[32]

• <u>You live for the moment</u>. You are always looking for the next thrill. You get bored quickly. You fall in love quickly. You fall out of love quickly. You are willing to do what will give you a thrill—even if this involves immoral or illegal activities.

  God's opinion of this: You are controlled by your feelings. You will never be satisfied. You will always have a continual lust for more.[33]

• <u>You are a spendthrift</u>. You often see new purchases as a way to bring pleasure—whether it's a pair of flip flops or a new car.

  God's opinion of this: You will become poor.[34]

---

calling out to those who pass by, who go straight on their way. "Let all who are simple come in here!" she says to those who lack judgment.

[30] 1 Corinthians 15:33: Do not be misled: "Bad company corrupts good character."

[31] 1 Samuel 16:7: But the LORD said to Samuel, "Do not consider his appearance or his height, for I have rejected him. The LORD does not look at the things man looks at. Man looks at the outward appearance, but the LORD looks at the heart."

[32] Proverbs 18:2: A fool finds no pleasure in understanding but delights in airing his own opinions.

[33] Ephesians 4:19: Having lost all sensitivity, they have given themselves over to sensuality so as to indulge in every kind of impurity, with a continual lust for more.

[34] Proverbs 21:17: He who loves pleasure will become poor; whoever loves wine and oil will never be rich.

- <u>You don't respond well to correction</u>. You view anyone who confronts you as the enemy. Being confronted isn't pleasurable, thus the person who lovingly tries to point out hurtful patterns in your life will always be seen as an adversary.

  God's opinion of this: You just want to be surrounded by people who flatter you and make you feel good about yourself. You call people who are really your enemies your friends, and people who are genuine friends, your enemies.[35]

- <u>You are unreliable</u>. You abandon commitments. You are surprised if anyone is upset that you don't keep a commitment when something more fun comes up.

  God's opinion of this: You lack integrity. I am faithful to all my promises, and I expect you to be faithful to your promises.[36]

What Others Experience

If you are a friend of a pleasure-oriented person, the following may be characteristic of your friendship.

<u>Your initial experience may be enjoyable</u>.
You will probably enjoy the beginning stages of your friendship with a pleasure-oriented friend. She'll always be thinking of fun things to do and be ready for the next adventure. She enjoys great food and good restaurants. She's always ready to see the next blockbuster movie or go to a party. She may have season tickets to the games of your favorite sports team. She may have the latest gadgets and a sporty car. She'll go bungee jumping, drag racing, or skydiving if they seem like fun to her, and she'll want you to come along. Your friend may be the life of the party.

Friendship with a pleasure-oriented friend will probably be most attractive to other pleasure-oriented friends. On the other hand, friendships with rightness-oriented friends will probably wear thin pretty quickly, because the pleasure-oriented friend will engage in activities that will cause

---

[35] Proverbs 27:6: Wounds from a friend can be trusted, but an enemy multiplies kisses.
[36] Psalm 145:13: The LORD is faithful to all his promises and loving toward all he has made. Proverbs 3:3-4: Let love and faithfulness never leave you; bind them around your neck, write them on the tablet of your heart. Then you will win favor and a good name in the sight of God and man.

disapproval from the rightness-oriented friend. When the rightness-oriented friend tries to adjure the pleasure-oriented friend to do what she thinks is right, the pleasure-oriented friend may respond angrily. The rightness-oriented friend will be told to mind her own business.

The protection-oriented friend will feel uncomfortable with the way the pleasure-oriented friend pushes the limits. Pushing the limits doesn't feel safe, so friendship between the two is not likely to prosper.

<u>You will be encouraged to be irresponsible</u>.
Pleasure-oriented friends will encourage you to live irresponsibly. So what if you can't afford to eat at Outback Steakhouse just put it on your credit card. So what if you need to get up early for work tomorrow, there's still time to play another game. So what if you promised to go to your Uncle Fred's 90th birthday party, going skiing will be lots more fun. And like sailors captured by the allure of the Sirens in Homer's *Odyssey*, you abandon what is the right course and head in the direction of pleasure.

<u>You will be tempted to become a fool</u>.
Ecclesiastes 7:4 announces that the heart of fools is in the house of pleasure. Friendship with a pleasure-oriented friend may tempt you to live for pleasure and become a fool. Living for pleasure has been tried before. Others have been there and done that. One guy who got sucked into pleasure-oriented living cynically asked, "What does pleasure accomplish?"[37] He concluded that pleasure is meaningless; pursuing pleasure yields about as much benefit as chasing after the wind.[38] Only a fool would stand in his backyard and chase after whatever breeze blows through the yard.

<u>You will be tempted to abandon good decisions and good character qualities</u>.

Because self-control limits living for the moment, your pleasure-oriented friend will be unlikely to be supportive as you seek to put on habits that bring pleasure to God. Whether it's your diet, your budget, your use of time, or your service—the pleasure-oriented friend will happily meddle

---

[37] Ecclesiastes 2:2: "Laughter," I said, "is foolish. And what does pleasure accomplish?"
[38] Ecclesiastes 2:11: Yet when I surveyed all that my hands had done and what I had toiled to achieve, everything was meaningless, a chasing after the wind; nothing was gained under the sun.

in any of these. She will push you to cross the line with her, and she will encourage you to use your resources for your pleasure, especially if as you use them, she benefits too.

You may sear your conscience.

The pleasure-oriented friend may make it easy for you to sear your conscience. By repeatedly crossing the line with her, the result will be a conscience that has become calloused and insensitive to bringing God pleasure.

You may accept puny delights and live a shallow life.

Rather than seeking to delight the One who has eternal pleasures at His right hand, you settle for puny delights that don't satisfy for more than a moment and grieve God. Seeking momentary pleasure instead of delighting in God is like:

- Eating a stale cookie for dessert rather than having a homemade piece of fresh caramel apple pie.

- Sleeping on a lumpy mattress in a worn out motel rather than staying at a 5-star resort.

- Listening to your favorite music artist on a scratched LP rather than hearing that same artist live and in concert.

It's puny rather than exhilarating. Sadly, pursuing these shallow joys circumvents experiencing the exhilaration of true joy.

You will be tempted to be envious and covetous.

Because living for pleasure creates a continual lust for more, friendship with a pleasure-oriented friend will tempt you to become greedy and dissatisfied. Since the latest and greatest innovations always promise to deliver more, like your pleasure-oriented friend, you may be discontent with what you have and want whatever new toy comes on the market. You snatch up the latest cell phone, the fastest computer, the newest video game only to learn that something newer, faster, and more fun has just arrived on the market.

You may become habitually angry.

Proverbs 22:24-25 warns about associating with a friend who is hot tempered and easily angered because you may learn her ways and get yourself ensnared. As you continually associate with a pleasure-oriented friend, and as she flies off the handle when her pleasure is thwarted, you may follow her example. Before you realize it, you are ensnared in angry habits. You find yourself exploding in anger. You are ashamed of your temper but feel powerless to change.

<u>You will be in danger of becoming a slave</u>.

Second Peter 2:19 warns that whatever we give ourselves to will enslave us. Friendship with a pleasure-oriented friend may cause you to become just as enslaved to pleasure as your friend—with the same disappointing result. Ephesians 4:19 promises that when we live to satisfy our senses, it never satisfies. Even though we earnestly seek to get satisfaction by indulging in every kind of impurity, we're always left dissatisfied and wanting more. We're never free of the desire for pleasure. It keeps us in its clutches, as a slave to every whim, and never satisfied.

Have you ever tried capturing a toy from one of those vending machines equipped with a mechanical claw and filled with stuffed animals. It seems that it would be simple to guide the claw to an enticing toy, maneuver the claw into position, and capture the prize. And so, you stuff quarters into the slot looking for an easy prize. Similarly, the pleasure-oriented friend believes pursuing pleasure will lead to an easy prize. Frustratingly, neither delivers on their seeming promise. Just as the consumer walks away from the vending machine empty handed, those who pursue pleasure walk away empty.

Like Samson, with his eyes gouged out and chained to a grinding wheel in prison, you become a slave to things that don't satisfy. You crave your next pleasure, you pursue your pleasure, you come away empty, and then you repeat the cycle. Another revolution around the grinding stone. You find yourself fitting the definition of insanity popularly attributed to Einstein: Doing the same thing over and over again and expecting different results. You pursue pleasure expecting it to deliver *this* time.

In the end, if you are a pleasure-oriented friend, you will miss the joy of having God as your friend. You will not love others properly. Your friendships will be shallow and inauthentic.

Chapter 9
The Comfort-Oriented Friend
Friends Who Crave Ease and Comfort

Heart's Desire

Imagine you have a friend with an abusive husband. One day when you drop by your friend's house she doesn't answer the door. Knowing that she is expecting you, you do just what every person does on television detective shows—you try the door handle and when it opens, you go into the house.

As you walk into the kitchen, you see your friend's husband beating her. Putting yourself in peril, you rescue your friend and see to it that her husband never abuses her again. You are so incensed by how you saw your friend treated that you become an advocate for battered wives. You testify at congressional hearings and are instrumental in getting legislation passed to help women in abusive relationships.

One day, while the friend you originally rescued is visiting you, she can't find any bottled water in the fridge. When she complains to you, you get water for her. A month later, after you have both come back from a lovely resort vacation, graciously arranged and paid for by a supporter of the legislation you worked on, your friend stays at your home overnight before leaving the following morning to return to her own home. When she doesn't find any food in the fridge, she again complains, grumbling that at least when she lived with her husband, they always had good food and plenty of it.

You are shocked! Your friend sounds just like the children of Israel after Moses led them out of slavery.

Moses' advocacy for the children of Israel was exemplary. Although he had grown up as the privileged adopted son of Pharaoh's daughter, he remained loyal to his fellow Israelites. Not only did he remain loyal, Moses chose to be mistreated with his fellow Jews rather than live like a prince in the palace. Have you ever had a friend like that? I'd choose Moses for a friend any day!

At age 40, Moses became so incensed when he saw an Egyptian slave driver beating an Israelite that he intervened and killed the Egyptian. Forced to flee the country, Moses later returned to deliver his people from Pharaoh and slavery at God's command.

Moses and his brother, Aaron, appealed to Pharaoh to let the Israelites go. Moses' advocacy was spurned by Pharaoh, but he persisted. As the plagues brought by God on the Egyptians became more and more terrible, Pharaoh became so furious that he issued a death warrant for Moses, stating that the day he saw Moses again was the day Moses would die.

Moses clearly was not a comfort-oriented friend. It's hard to imagine anyone being a better friend than Moses.

Sadly, the same cannot be said for the children of Israel. They apparently were such comfort-oriented people that Moses' exemplary friendship meant little to them. Over and over again we see the Israelites complaining and grumbling against Moses when things weren't comfortable.

Within days of crossing the Red Sea on dry ground as God miraculously parted the waters for the Israelites and then closed the sea back up to kill the pursuing enemy, the Israelites were angry at Moses. In spite of the fact that three days earlier the people had put their trust in the Lord and

His servant Moses, when their comfort was threatened by lack of water, the Israelites complained against Moses. "What are we to drink?" they grumbled.

Rather than screaming at them for being such ingrates, Moses asked God for help and followed the Lord's instruction so that the people were provided with water. Moses continued to show genuine friendship to these comfort-oriented friends.

Moses then led them to the resort provided by God at Elim, where there were twelve springs and scores of palm trees. But shortly after leaving the resort, these comfort-oriented friends were again hot and bothered. Again they complained against Moses. The Israelites made the ludicrous statement that they wished they could have died in Egypt, because in Egypt they had all the food they wanted.

Still today, comfort-oriented friends care a lot about their comfort; they care little about friendship. Their hearts are drawn to friendships that are easy and convenient. A comfort-oriented friend is self-indulgent and loves to relax with friends who are not troublesome and who enjoy what she enjoys.

Acceptable Cost

What are some of the ways a comfort-oriented friend is willing to disrespect God and others in order to worship her idol of comfort? The comfort-oriented friend disrespects God by refusing to be self-controlled, self-disciplined, or diligent. Instead she quits when things get hard (coming up with seemingly very good reasons why she shouldn't continue), or she refuses to get involved. She is glad God sacrificed His Son for her, but she's not interested in showing the same level of friendship to Him or others.

The comfort-oriented friend disrespects others (including God) by grumbling and complaining. She doesn't care that her grumbling and complaining aren't fun to hear. She doesn't care that her speech is not edifying. She praises her idol of comfort with speech that is disgruntled and fault finding. It is through bellyaching and griping that she worships her idol. Grumbling and complaining are her psalms of praise to the idol of comfort.

The comfort-oriented friend is willing to sacrifice maturity. In James 1:2-4, God explains that persevering in trials leads to maturity. This friend is happy to be immature. She quits when given the opportunity to persevere and grow. Like a toddler who refuses to walk, preferring to be carried, the comfort-oriented friend doesn't mind making other people carry the load.

Pointing out the benefits of perseverance and diligence won't motivate the comfort-oriented friend. If you entice her with a marriage that sings—she'll find it's not worth the effort. If you entice her with a job that challenges and provides growth opportunities—she'll decide it's too hard. If you entice her with friendships that spur her on to godliness—she's not interested. The comfort-oriented friend is willing to sacrifice everything at the altar of comfort.

Nightmare/Fear

Let's consider the nightmares, dislikes, pet peeves, and fears of a comfort-oriented friend. See if you can answer the following multiple choice quiz about her nightmares, dislikes, pet peeves, and fears.

1. Which of the following would probably cause nightmares for a comfort-oriented friend?
   a. Friends who are lazy.
   b. Friends with high expectations, who encourage her to grow.
   c. Friends who aren't part of the "in" group.
   d. Losing the approval of a friend because she always complains.

2. Which of the following would probably show up on a list of pet peeves for a comfort-oriented friend?
   a. Being asked to help clean up after an event rather than simply attending and enjoying it.
   b. Having someone show up for a baby shower who didn't RSVP.
   c. Being asked to pray in front of a group at lunch.
   d. Being on a volleyball team with someone who just wants to have fun and doesn't care about winning.

3. Which of the following would a comfort-oriented friend most dislike?
   a. Having someone who is socially awkward loudly acknowledge her in public.

   b.   Having a needy friend who frequently wants help.

   c.   Being asked regularly by an approval-oriented friend, "Are you upset with me?"

   d.   Having a control-oriented friend who never lets her be the leader.

4. Which of the following would a comfort-oriented friend be most likely to fear?

   a.   Having someone be one up on her.

   b.   Not being noticed by the right people.

   c.   Being stuck with someone who won't follow the rules.

   d.   Being deprived of something considered necessary for her comfort.[39]

Being deprived of comfort is so distasteful that a comfort-oriented friend would consider murder. This sounds farfetched, but that is exactly what the Israelites were ready to do to Moses. When the children of Israel didn't have water in Exodus 17, they began eyeing rocks in preparation for stoning Moses. Clearly, murder is extreme, and it's hard to think of everyday examples. However, since God's word openly states that all of us are like the rest of us, we should probably anticipate that even if we never see anger at being deprived of comfort translated into murder, it is likely that sinful anger is a regular occurrence in the heart of the comfort-oriented friend. This may not seem like a big deal until we hear what Christ says in Matthew 5:21-22:

> *You have heard that it was said to the people long ago, "Do not murder, and anyone who murders will be subject to judgment. But I tell you that anyone who is angry with his brother will be subject to judgment.*

God equates sinful anger with murder.

> *Anyone who hates his brother is a murderer, and you know that no murderer has eternal life in him (1 John 3:15).*

Seen in Action

Let's walk through a typical day with a comfort-oriented friend.

---

[39] 1b, 2a, 3b, 4d

<u>Friday</u>

7:10 am   Rose hits the snooze alarm for the fourth time. She had planned to get up at 6:30, but she just wants a few minutes longer to sleep.

7:18 am   Rose is aroused to wakefulness when her husband, Rich, gently kisses her goodbye before he leaves for work. Looking at the clock, Rose jumps out of bed and races to get ready for work. She knows Rich wishes she would make the bed in the morning, but she'll be late to work again if she makes the bed now.

8:11 am   Late, even though she didn't make the bed, Rose crams her purse into her desk and heads to the office kitchenette to get coffee. Phyllis is there and they talk for 20 minutes before Rose heads back to her desk.

10:23 am   Rose gets on Facebook and uploads her pictures from last weekend's three day vacation in Chicago with Rich.

10:53 am   Rose logs off Facebook. She has a staff meeting at 11.

12:08 pm   "You don't look happy. What's up?" asks Beth as they ride the elevator to the basement cafeteria.

           "Ralph just told me that they're changing the venue for the board meeting next week," complains Rose. "They're going to use the South Street location instead of the Central Avenue building. Now I'll have to contact all the board members. I wish they'd think of those things ahead of time. I told Ralph that I wouldn't be able to get his report done today since I'm going to have to make all those calls."

12:25 pm   Beth and Rose put their lunch trays on an empty table and sit down to eat.

           "That banana cream pie looks good," Beth comments.

           "I couldn't pass it up," Rose responds. "Banana cream is one of my favorites. My diet can wait until tomorrow. Besides, I'm helping Cheryl and Ford move tomorrow. I'm sure that will burn off some calories."

"When are we going to do our spa weekend?" Beth questions.

"We probably should have gone this weekend, since Rich is taking his scout troop camping. I think they're going again the first weekend in August. Want to do it then?" Rose answers.

"That sounds okay to me. Shall I see if Marney and Kathy can go that weekend?" Beth asks.

"Sure, that would be great," Rose replies. "Do you want to make the hotel reservations for us after you talk to them?"

4:45 pm Rose puts on her coat and leaves for the weekend. She knows she's leaving early, but she wants to get home before Rich leaves to take the scouts camping.

5:14 pm Rose drops her coat on the couch and looks for Rich. He's in the garage putting their tent in the back of his Honda.

"What time will you be back tomorrow?" Rose asks.

"I think I should be home around 3. What are your plans?"

"Tonight I'm going over to Samantha's to watch movies. Then tomorrow I'm planning to help Cheryl and Ford move," Rose responds.

As Rich continues stowing camping gear in the trunk, Rose continues, "Hey, do you remember me asking you about us being sponsors for the junior/senior year-end banquet? I talked to Jan on Facebook today and found out they expect us to not only go to the banquet, but they also expect us to help tear down. I thought we just had to go to the banquet. If I had known we had to help tear down, I never would have agreed that we would help them."

7:10 pm   Rose rummages through her pantry to find something to take to Samantha's movie night. On the top shelf she finds some stale Christmas candy that nobody liked. She decides to take that.

7:38 pm   Samantha introduces Rose to Belle. Rose has seen Belle in church the last couple months but hasn't introduced herself. Rose converses briefly with Belle and then goes to snag the recliner for the movie. She doesn't want to get stuck sitting on the floor.

11:30 pm   At the conclusion of the second chick flick, Rose carries her plate to the kitchen and puts it on the counter. She knows she probably ought to stay and help clean-up but since she's helping Cheryl and Ford move tomorrow, she wants to go home and go to bed.

<u>Saturday</u>
9:15 am   Rose hits the snooze alarm again. The moving party was scheduled to start at 9 am. Oh well, it looked like Cheryl and Ford had plenty of people signed up to help. This is really Rose's only day to sleep in anyway. Maybe she can drop by later and help Cheryl unpack.

Perhaps you have friends like Rose. Perhaps you *are* Rose. Let's consider what God might say to the Rose's of this world when He observes the characteristics often found in comfort-oriented friends.

- <u>You complain frequently.</u> You make comments like, "If I had known this was going to happen, I would never have gotten into this," or "This isn't what I signed up for."

   God's opinion of this: You are a grumbler. When the children of Israel grumbled I sent a destroying angel. What makes you think I would find it acceptable now?

- <u>You don't reach out to new people.</u> Because reaching out to new people requires moving out of your comfort zone, you don't reach out. It's easier to let someone else do it. You are complacently happy with your circle of friends. You wait for others to reach out to you.

God's opinion of this: You are just like the folks in Sodom, unconcerned about others. Do you remember what I did to them? Do you need a reminder like the reminder I gave the Israelites in Ezekiel 16:49-50? *"Now this was the sin of your sister Sodom: She and her daughters were arrogant, overfed and <u>unconcerned</u>; they did not help the poor and needy. They were haughty and did detestable things before me. Therefore I did away with them as you have seen."* (Emphasis added.)

- <u>You start well, but you don't finish</u>. You don't follow through.

God's opinion of this: You are just like the lazy man in Proverbs 12:27.[40] You begin well but you don't finish what you start. You will be immature until you learn to persevere. Maturity comes as you persevere (James 1:2-4).

- <u>You tend to be complacent</u>. You are satisfied with the status quo.

God's opinion of this: The complacency of fools will destroy them (Proverbs 1:32).

- <u>You have little concern for the unsaved</u>. As long as they don't interfere with your comfort, you don't give much thought to those who don't know God.

God's opinion of this: You are unloving. This is how I showed my love: I sent my one and only Son into the world that you might live through him. Since I so loved you, you also ought to love one another (1 John 4:9, 11).

- <u>You always have a reason for why you can't do something hard</u>. You are good at making others seem unreasonable if they expect you to work hard.

God's opinion of this: You are like the sluggard in Proverbs 26:13. You are full of good excuses, which I find unacceptable. I didn't accept excuses from Adam and Eve in the garden; I won't accept them from you either.

---

[40] Proverbs 12:27: The lazy man does not roast his game, but the diligent man prizes his possessions.

- <u>You are not dependable</u>. You say you'll do something, but it never seems to get done. You encourage people to put confidence in you, but then you let them down.

  God's opinion of this: You are like vinegar to the teeth and smoke to the eyes (Proverbs 10:26). These are not qualities people want in friends.

- <u>You make soft little choices</u>. So what if you didn't call last night as you said you would. So what if you're a little late. So what if you didn't make it to Bible study this week. One week won't hurt. It's hard to convince you that these soft little choices are wrong because it seems like others are making a mountain out of a molehill.

  God's opinion of this: Your soft little choices will destroy you. Do you remember what I said in Proverbs 6:10-11? *"A little sleep, a little slumber, a little folding of the hands to rest—and poverty will come on you like a bandit and scarcity like an armed man. "*

  The only thing this person wanted was just a *little* sleep (one more time hitting the snooze alarm), a *little* more slumber; just a *little* time to rest. However, poverty will come like a robber. A robber comes with no warning. You think everything is okay and then a robber shows up and takes everything you have. Scarcity will come like an armed man. When an armed man puts a gun in your back and holds you up, you're powerless. You need to understand that's what going to happen to you. When you're not expecting it, poverty is going to overtake you and it's going to be too strong to overpower.

What Others Experience

<u>Your initial experience may be enjoyable</u>.

Being around a comfort-oriented friend is fairly easy in the beginning. She doesn't seem like she'll impose expectations, and its okay with her if you stay in your comfort zone. Because she loves comfort, you may have to be the one who initiates the friendship. The comfort-oriented friend will probably not invest the effort to reach out to you. However, if you break the ice and get the ball rolling, you can expect the comfort-oriented friend to respond positively.

If you are a pleasure-oriented friend, you'll usually find that a comfort-oriented friend is happy to be your friend. Pursuing pleasure is often easy. Because of this, pleasure-oriented and comfort-oriented friends are like cousins, with a definite family resemblance. However, while the payoff in pleasure motivates the pleasure-oriented friend to invest effort to achieve pleasure, the same is not true for a comfort-oriented friend. She loves pleasure that is easily attained. She will probably be happy to watch movies with you, but she will be less likely to go camping with you. Camping may require too much work for a comfort-oriented friend.

The comfort-oriented friend will probably not be drawn to you if you are a control-oriented friend or a rightness-oriented friend. Friendship with control-oriented or rightness-oriented friends is too demanding.

The comfort-oriented friend leaves the serving and hard tasks to you.

After you have been friends for a while, it begins to dawn on you that your comfort-oriented friend lets you do the serving in your relationship. She lets you clean up after dinner, call people to organize events, make reservations when you go out to eat, and figure out the directions when you travel somewhere.

You often find that things don't go smoothly when your friend is in charge because she doesn't invest the effort required to plan ahead. She leaves things until the last minute and does just enough to get by.

You have to listen to her complain.

You routinely hear your comfort-oriented friend complain. Her complaints generally revolve around how she has been inconvenienced. Somebody didn't wait on her fast enough at McDonald's; someone didn't cook the meatloaf right and it is dry; the weather is miserable; the neighbor's dog is barking; someone called during the last 10 minutes of her favorite show; the copier paper is not where it's supposed to be; she didn't get a big enough raise and on and on. She ignores God's command in Philippians 2:14 to do everything without complaining or arguing. If she thought about that verse at all, she'd probably complain that the command was too hard to keep.

The comfort-oriented friend believes she is being open and transparent by telling you what she doesn't like. She believes that sharing her complaints is admirable, not repugnant. She fails to realize that she has ignored

Ephesians 4:29. You are not encouraged or built up by your comfort-oriented friend, you are dumped on.

You find it easy to pander to your friend's desire for comfort.

Because the comfort-oriented friend regularly complains, you may find it easy to refrain from asking for her help. It's easier to ask for help from someone who won't complain. It's easier to just let her be lazy.

You can't depend on her.

You may find that your comfort-oriented friend is undependable. When group projects are assigned in history class, you don't want her to be part of your group. When the group divides up the workload, guess whose part never get's done? Although she promises she'll have it done, you end up getting a D+ because she doesn't follow through.

She may enthusiastically agree to new ideas or projects. However, when she realizes these commitments will require time and energy, she tends to back out. Since the comfort-oriented friend is inclined to abandon things requiring effort, you may find she is untrustworthy.

Problems aren't solved.

Expending the energy and effort required to solve problems is disagreeable to the comfort-oriented friend. Although she may be aware of the instruction in Matthew 5:24 to go and be reconciled, she ignores this. She would rather claim that she doesn't have a problem than have to go solve it. If a problem gets solved, it will likely only happen if you persistently pursue solving it.

You are tempted to become comfort-oriented.

You may be tempted to become like your comfort-oriented friend. Your friend will encourage you to put off chores to watch a movie, make phone calls tomorrow so you can stay longer and visit, go shopping now rather than clean your house.

You may be tempted to become just as irresponsible as your friend. She doesn't push you to excel. She doesn't care if you grow in godliness. The end result of your friendship may be that you stop growing spiritually. You become like your comfort-oriented friend. Friendship with a comfort-oriented friend isn't genuine and authentic. This friend loves herself, not God and others.

Chapter 10
The Prestige-Oriented Friend
Friends Who Want to Climb the Status Ladder

Even if we've never read *The Three Musketeers*, most of us know the motto by which these swashbuckling friends lived: "All for one, one for all." Written 1800 years after Christ's death,[41] this was not a motto that would have appealed to Christ's disciples before His death.

At the time of Christ's death, His friends were absorbed in who would be greatest. This was so important to them that even when Christ told them that in a very short time He would be betrayed, mocked, flogged, and crucified, his friends simply saw it as an opportunity for advancement.

Imagine if you were to tell your colleagues at work that you have been diagnosed with a terminal disease and have been given just a few weeks to live. You may not have any idea how your colleagues will respond to your announcement, but since you have been a tight-knit group, you want to prepare them for your impending death. Would you be shocked if they responded like Christ's disciples responded? Would you be shocked if

---

[41] Published 1844-45.

your colleagues started coming to you privately, asking if they could have your corner office? How would you react if one of them even had his mom call to chat with you and try to influence you in favor of her son? Do you think no one would ever be that crass?

> *Now as Jesus was going up to Jerusalem, he took the twelve disciples aside and said to them, "We are going up to Jerusalem, and the Son of Man will be betrayed to the chief priests and the teachers of the law. They will condemn him to death and will turn him over to the Gentiles to be mocked and flogged and crucified. On the third day he will be raised to life!"*
>
> *Then the mother of Zebedee's sons came to Jesus with her sons and, kneeling down, asked a favor of him.*
>
> *"What is it you want?" he asked.*
>
> *She said, "Grant that one of these two sons of mine may sit at your right and the other at your left in your kingdom"* (Matthew 20:17-21).

Heart's Desire

The prestige-oriented friend is all about her status and reputation. She will look for friends who can serve as stepping stones in garnering more prominence and position.

The heart's desire of the friend who wants to climb the status ladder is to be respected and recognized by others. The prestige-oriented friend will tend to choose as friends only those who can advance her status or those who will be impressed by her status.

Prestige-oriented friends highly value being part of the "in group" and having others admire them because they belong to the "right" group. This group may be composed of fashionable people, wealthy and professionally successful people, politically successful people, beautiful, witty, and powerful people, athletically gifted people—you get the picture. When the prestige-oriented friend doesn't belong to the group she has earmarked as the "in group," her friendships will revolve around networking to give her entry into her desired group.

Sadly, the heart of the prestige-oriented friend is ruled by pride. She loves for others to put her on a pedestal and look up to her. She *adorns* herself with pride. Like a debutante preparing herself for a ball, she bedecks herself with a necklace of arrogance, earrings of conceit, and a tiara of haughtiness.

Acceptable Costs

Once she has gained entrance into the group she wants, the friend who wants to climb the status ladder will see little reason to be loyal to those who may have helped her attain her social rank. The prestige-oriented friend will not want to have as friends those who are not socially acceptable or prestigious. She may not care if those beneath her see her as a gold digger, ladder climber, or apple polisher, as long as she is accepted by those in what she regards as the "in group."

When James and John went after the most prestigious positions in Christ's kingdom, they knew the other disciples would probably be upset with them. Christ's disciples had already gotten into scuffles prior to this about who would be greatest. Nevertheless, James and John were so completely focused on their desire for prestige, it mattered little what others thought. Humility and meekness were thrown under the bus in their ambition to be first.

Nightmare/Fear

Haman was in high spirits. All his dreams seemed to be coming true. He had just attended an exclusive banquet and was invited to another one the next day. Life didn't get much better than that—an invitation to a banquet with the king and queen to which no one else was invited. Haman was so happy he couldn't wait to tell all his friends and family. He was looking forward to boasting to them about all the ways the king had honored him and how the king had elevated him above the other nobles and officials.

But Haman's delight was spoiled by a nightmare in the form of Mordecai. Mordecai wouldn't kneel down to Haman or pay him honor. For a man who loved prestige as Haman did, this was infuriating. Mordecai's lack of respect had the power to spoil all of Haman's happiness—even being invited to an exclusive banquet couldn't overcome the nightmare of not being shown the respect he wanted.

Unknown to Haman, his nightmare was about to go on steroids. It all started one night when the king couldn't fall asleep. The king got up and ordered the book of the chronicles, the record of his reign, to be brought in and read to him. It was found recorded there that Mordecai had exposed a couple of Secret Service officers, who had conspired to assassinate King Xerxes.

"What honor and recognition has Mordecai received for this?" the king asked.

"Nothing has been done for him," his attendants answered.

The king said, "Who is in the court?" Now Haman had just entered the outer court of the palace to speak to the king about hanging Mordecai on the gallows he had erected for him.

His attendants answered, "Haman is standing in the court."

"Bring him in," the king ordered.

When Haman entered, the king asked him, "What should be done for the man the king delights to honor?"

Now Haman thought to himself, "Who is there that the king would rather honor than me?" So he answered the king, "For the man the king delights to honor, have them bring a royal robe the king has worn and a horse the king has ridden, one with a royal crest placed on its head. Then let the robe and horse be entrusted to one of the king's most noble princes. Let them robe the man the king delights to honor, and lead him on the horse through the city streets, proclaiming before him, 'This is what is done for the man the king delights to honor!'"

"Go at once," the king commanded Haman. "Get the robe and the horse and do just as you have suggested for Mordecai the Jew, who sits at the king's gate. Do not neglect anything you have recommended."

So Haman did as he was told and got the robe and the horse. He robed Mordecai, and led him on horseback through the city streets, proclaiming before him, "This is what is done for the man the king delights to honor!"

Afterward Mordecai returned to the king's gate. But Haman rushed home, with his head covered in grief.[42]

---

[42] Esther 6:1-12. Esther 6:2 actually reads: It was found recorded there that Mordecai

Like Haman, the prestige-oriented friend considers it nightmarish if she is not respected as she thinks she should be. Similarly, she finds it a nightmare to be viewed as an outcast or misfit, as unworthy of belonging to her chosen group, or undesirable. She fears being disgraced or not being accepted.

A friend who wants to climb the ladder of status hates to be ignored or treated with indifference. She loathes being treated as if she doesn't matter or as if she is not important. She doesn't want to be seen as common; she considers herself superior.

Seen in Action

Let's follow a prestige-oriented friend through a typical day.

9:02 am   Sheena Kennedy's husband, Anthony, steps into her home office. Directly across from him is a wall lined with plaques, diplomas, and certificates earned by Sheena, now nicely framed and hung on her trophy wall.

"What time did you want to leave for the Health and Fun Fair," Anthony queries. "Our shift at the information booth starts at 10:30."

"I'll be ready to leave as soon as I finish putting our Health and Fun Fair schedule on Twitter," Sheena responds.

10:00 am   As Sheena and Anthony arrive at the Health and Fun Fair, which was organized to raise funds for the local hospital, Sheena reminds Anthony that the governor is planning to attend, and she has asked the hospital administrator to introduce them.

10:15 am   Sheena sees Dr. Washington and his wife and walks over to greet them. Dr. Washington is a renowned neurosurgeon, and Sheena certainly wants everyone to see that Dr. Washington knows who she is. They chat for a few minutes, and then Sheena and Anthony head for the information booth. On their way to the booth, Dr. Washington's secretary sees Sheena

had exposed Bigthana and Teresh, two of the king's officers who guarded the doorway, who had conspired to assassinate King Xerxes.

and yells, "Hi, Girlfriend!"   Sheena acknowledges her but doesn't stop to say hi. In fact, she is a bit offended that Dr. Washington's secretary would act like they are friends.

11:22 am   Mercy Kincaid, the president of the company where Anthony works, stops to say hello to the Kennedys. She imparts the good news that her husband, Howard, was released from the hospital yesterday. Howard had been rushed to the emergency room when he began experiencing shortness of breath two nights ago. Because Howard's family has a history of heart disease, everyone feared he might be having a heart attack. Mercy tells the Kennedys that, after running some tests, the doctors determined Howard's heart is fine.

12:15 pm   Amy comes to the Health and Fun Fare information booth with her arms loaded with carry out cartons from Chili's. "Hi, Sheena! Hi, Anthony! I knew your shift didn't end until 2:30 so I thought I'd bring you lunch. How's it going?"

"We're having a great time," Sheena enthuses. "Based on the folks we've gotten to talk to, it seems like a lot of people have come out to support the hospital. We've talked to..." and Sheena reels off a list of the city's wealthiest residents and community leaders.

12:27 pm   As Amy leaves the information booth, Sheena comments to Anthony, "I feel sorry for Amy. She tries so hard to dress right, but she always seems to be about two years behind everyone else."

1:18 pm   Mercy brings the chairman of the American Medical Association over to the information booth to get instructions for the event he is judging. They chat for several minutes. Wanting to impress the AMA chairman with her relationship with Mercy, Sheena asks Mercy in a solicitous tone, "How is Howard?" Mercy looks a bit puzzled as she replies, "Howard is fine."

2:03 pm   A camera crew from Channel 24 shows up looking for someone to interview about the Heath and Fun Fair. Sheena volunteers to be filmed. In the interview, Sheena makes it sound as if she is one of the event organizers, not simply a volunteer. She makes sure to mention talking with the governor.

3:15pm   Before she and Anthony leave, Sheena goes around thanking everyone for helping, as if she were in charge and they volunteered to serve her.

3:45 pm   Sheena puts her camera appearance on Facebook and Twitter as soon as she gets home.

6:07 pm   Anthony and Sheena meet friends for dinner. Sheena subtly weaves into the conversation all the prominent people she interacted with at the Health and Fun Fair.

9:37 pm   Sheena texts several of her friends to remind them she will be on the 10:00 news.

10:00 pm Sheena turns on the local news so that she can catch the segment for which she was interviewed.

Perhaps you have friends like Sheena. Perhaps you *are* Sheena. Let's consider what God might say to the Sheena's of this world when He observes the characteristics often found in prestige-oriented friends.

- <u>You are careful to make sure everyone knows you, especially the right people</u>. You position yourself to be around the right people or meet the right people.

  God's opinion of this: You are losing your reward from Me.[43] Is that what you want? Would you really prefer to have the puny rewards I allow people to give you rather than the magnificent rewards I can give you?

- <u>You are dissatisfied if you are put in obscure service positions</u>. You think you should be put in prominent positions.

---

[43] Matthew 6:1: "Be careful not to do your 'acts of righteousness' before men, to be seen by them. If you do, you will have no reward from your Father in heaven.

God's opinion of this: You have an inflated view of your abilities—who gave them to you and why.[44]   Those who insist on being first will end up in last place.[45]

- <u>You are boastful</u>. You like to make sure everyone knows how great you are. You are eager to have people know what you are doing. You are eager to talk about yourself. In order not to appear crass you may try to disguise your boasting. For example, you may make your boast sound like a complaint, "These black tie affairs get old after a while" or like a prayer request, "I've got a meeting with the mayor tomorrow. Please pray things go well." However, even subtle boasting is still boasting.

  God's opinion of this: You're boasting about the wrong person. You should be boasting about Me, not boasting about yourself. You are seeking your own honor. Rather than gaining honor, prepare to be disgraced.[46]

- <u>You use flattery to gain friends</u>. You praise others simply to make them well disposed toward you so that you can get something from them.

  God's opinion of this: You have misunderstood how to gain favor. He who rebukes a man will in the end gain more favor than he who has a flattering tongue (Proverbs 28:23). Instead, you are like the folks in Jude 16: *"These men are grumblers and faultfinders; they follow their own evil desires; they boast about themselves and flatter others for their own advantage."*

- <u>You love to be praised</u>. You like to be put on a pedestal. You love to be complimented and admired. You look for positions and opportunities to give you the praise and admiration of others.

---

[44] 1 Corinthians 4:7: For who makes you different from anyone else? What do you have that you did not receive? And if you did receive it, why do you boast as though you did not?

[45] Matthew 20:16: "So the last will be first, and the first will be last."

[46] 2 Corinthians 10:17-18: But, "Let him who boasts boast in the Lord." For it is not the one who commends himself who is approved, but the one whom the Lord commends. Proverbs 11:2: When pride comes, then comes disgrace, but with humility comes wisdom.

God's opinion of this: You are like the Pharisees in Matthew 23:6; they loved the place of honor at banquets and the most important seats in the synagogues. Like the Pharisees, you are going about getting honor the wrong way. I am the one who bestows favor and honor (Psalm 84:11). I have put honor in the hands of wisdom (Proverbs 3:16).[47] Esteem her and she will honor you (Proverbs 4:8). However, you don't seem to be interested in this path to honor. You are esteeming yourself and seeking your own honor. You want honor, but you are acting in a dishonorable way (Proverbs 25:27).

- <u>You are offended if you're not treated with proper dignity</u>. Being disrespected makes you furious. You demand respect from others. You are depressed and inconsolable if someone else receives an honor you think you should have gotten.

  God's opinion of this: You are acting like Haman acted in the book of Esther. I put Haman's biography in the Bible as an example to keep you from making the same choices.[48] Please heed my warning and profit from his biography.

- <u>You show partiality</u>. You don't show respect for those you consider beneath you. On the other hand, you are very respectful, even flattering to those you consider higher in rank. You show favoritism.

  God's opinion of this: To show partiality is not good.[49] You have become a judge with evil thoughts.[50]

- <u>You delight in airing your opinion</u>. You don't listen carefully to others. You are quick to jump into a conversation and express your view.

  God's opinion of this: A fool finds no pleasure in understanding but delights in airing his own opinions (Proverbs 18:2). When you air your opinion, you're usually the only person who thinks you're wise. Everyone around you thinks you're a fool.

---

[47] Proverbs 3:16: Long life is in her right hand; in her left hand are riches and honor.

[48] 1 Corinthians 10:11: These things happened to them as examples and were written down as warnings for us, on whom the fulfillment of the ages has come.

[49] Proverbs 28:21: To show partiality is not good—yet a man will do wrong for a piece of bread.

[50] James 2:4: have you not discriminated among yourselves and become judges with evil thoughts?

- <u>You think you're something</u>. You think you've earned your status and prestige.

  God's opinion of this: If anyone thinks he is something when he is nothing, he deceives himself (Galatians 6:3). You are deluded.

What Others Experience
<u>Your initial experience may be enjoyable.</u>

Just as the friends of celebrities are often accorded celebrity status, the same thing may occur in a friendship with a prestige-oriented friend. Since we are often known by the friends we keep, some of the status of a prestige-oriented friend may rub off on us like chalk off a chalkboard. It's nice to be held in high esteem. Thus, friendship with a prestige-oriented friend may be enjoyable for a time.

The person perhaps most attracted to a prestige-oriented friend is another prestige-oriented friend. Both initially enjoy the status achieved by the other.

<u>You must look right to be accepted.</u>

You may find that a prestige-oriented friend is unwilling to proffer friendship if you don't look right, belong to a desirable social group, have the right income, or have athletic talents. Without the right qualities, you are of little value to a friend who wants to climb the status ladder.

<u>You are encouraged to focus on character qualities which lead to prestige.</u>

By becoming friends with a person who is concerned about status, you may be tempted to focus on the same external characteristics on which she focuses. Beauty, wealth, athletic ability, or material possessions may become increasingly important to you. Simultaneously, qualities which produce true beauty are downgraded. Gentleness, goodness, self-control, and patience don't seem as attractive as they once did. Character qualities that were akin to blue chip stocks get downgraded to junk bond status. You become increasingly shallow.

<u>Your friend tempts you to compete.</u>

A desire for prestige leads naturally to seeking to be better than others. Since a prestige-oriented friend regularly competes to be first, you may find yourself sucked into a competition you didn't know you signed up for.

Suddenly, you too are jockeying for position and seeking for the prize of the highest honor.

Quarrels become routine for you.

To quote Proverbs 13:10, *"pride only breeds quarrels."* The prestige-oriented friend's desire for prestige may breed repeated quarrels. If you are her friend, expect to be involved in arguments. If you take her side, you'll find yourself quarreling with her opponents; if you don't take her side, you'll find yourself quarreling with her.

You are tempted to be jealous and envious.

Having a friend who is all about prestige may tempt you to envy her status. You forget what the end result will be for the status oriented friend, and look only at the status she currently enjoys. But like someone who maxed out her credit cards purchasing the latest toys and gadgets, the bills run up in accruing status will eventually come due. The status-oriented friend will find that God will not be mocked and that He will not give His glory to another. Pride goes before a fall, and the future of the status-oriented friend includes a fall.

You find your prestige-oriented friend's interest in you is not genuine.

At some point in your friendship with this person, you may perceive that she lacks a genuine interest in you. You may discover that if there is no payoff for interest in you, the prestige-oriented friend loses interest in the friendship. If you can't provide some sort of social advancement, if it doesn't help her prestige to be seen with you, then her interest in you disappears.

You may also realize that any expressed interest is fake. Like Mercy, who was asked by Sheena how her husband was doing in front of the president of the American Medical Association after Mercy had already shared the news that Howard was doing well, you may find that your prestige-oriented friend expresses interest in you or compassion for you to make herself look good in the eyes of someone she wants to impress.

When you learn that her interest is not genuine, you may feel as if you have been used. It may become apparent that her friendship was a sham. What you thought was friendship was nothing more than an advancement opportunity for your friend.

<u>You are tempted to become bitter</u>.

When you realize that your prestige-oriented friend has used you to advance her social status, you may be tempted to become bitter. It may leave a sour taste in your mouth to discover that your friendship was merely a stepping stone for her ambition.

In the end you realize your friendship was not genuine or authentic. The friend who wants to climb the ladder of status loves herself, not God and others.

Chapter 11
Getting Relationships Right

Perhaps the preceding chapters have been rough on you. Perhaps you saw glimpses of yourself in Ellie, Emily, or Rose. Perhaps you realized that you're similar to Victoria, Sophie, or Sheena. Maybe you're a carbon copy of Justine.

Perhaps you didn't see yourself in any of these women, but you know that if you're honest about your heart—your motives, your desires, and your ambitions—the picture of your heart is not the picture of a heart committed to loving God with all your soul and strength; nor does your heart reflect loving your neighbor as yourself.

Remember, everything we do comes from our heart, because the heart is the wellspring of our life. Every relationship we have is shaped by our heart. Thus far, we've painted what the canvas looks like when the heart is ruled by corrupt desires—approval, control, protection, rightness, pleasure, comfort, and prestige. The overriding conclusion we've reached is that the picture of a corrupt heart is ugly—and the friendships that grow out of a corrupt heart are ugly as well.

The good news is that the demolition team has finished its work, and we're ready for the construction process to begin. In the upcoming chapters we're going to review each friendship orientation and see what friendships look like when we do a U-turn, a radical change in direction. We're going to see what friendships look like when they become genuine and authentic.

As in any building endeavor, we need to make sure we lay a good foundation. The proper foundation in friendships is making sure we pick the right "best friend."

Finding the Right Best Friend

Consider this statement by C. S. Lewis:

> When I have learnt to love God better than my earthly [best friends], I shall love my earthly [best friends] better than I do now. In so far as I learn to love my earthly [best friends] at the expense of God and instead of God, I shall be moving towards the state in which I shall not love my earthly [best friends] at all. When first things are put first, second things are not suppressed but increased.[51]

Chew on this for a few moments. Lewis is saying you have to get the foundation right or the walls won't stand. Lewis is saying that if you get your priorities out of line, you lose everything and if we try to leave God out of the picture, we might as well not bother putting paint on the canvas.

This makes perfect sense to us when we're following a recipe. Suppose you decide to fix meatloaf for dinner tomorrow. The recipe has 3 simple steps.
1. Put 1 ½ pounds hamburger in a mixing bowl.
2. Add ketchup, salt, egg, and oatmeal and mix thoroughly.
3. Form into a loaf and bake at 350 degrees for 1 ½ hours.

As you assemble your ingredients you realize you have everything you need but the hamburger. Looking at your watch, you place a quick call

---

[51] Lewis, C. S., *Letters of C.S. Lewis* (New York: Harcourt Brace Jovanovich, 1966), p. 248, as quoted in Lane, Tim & Tripp, Paul, *Relationships: A Mess Worth Making* (Greensboro, NC: New Growth Press, 2006), p. 8.

to your husband and ask him to pick up the hamburger on his way home from work.

As you read back through the recipe, you see that the meatloaf needs to be in the oven for 1 ½ hours. If you wait until your husband gets home with the meat to finish your prep and cook the meatloaf, you won't be able to make it to your daughter's piano recital by 6 pm.

Time for Plan B. You decide to speed things up by cooking the meatloaf ingredients—without the hamburger—in advance, so that you'll already have step 3 done when your husband arrives home with the hamburger.

So, you preheat the oven, and mix the ketchup, salt, egg, and oatmeal. After greasing your pan, you add the ketchup mixture, form it into a loaf, and stick the mixture into the oven, setting the timer for 1 ½ hours.

Obviously, Plan B will be a colossal failure. Adding raw hamburger to cooked ketchup won't produce edible meatloaf. Loving our earthly best friends at the expense of God will also result in colossal failure. We'll end up with an unappealing mess that resembles ketchup and egg baked for 90 minutes. Eat it if you wish, but don't expect it to be savory.

We need to choose God as our best friend. If we don't, we won't be able to get any other friendship right. If we do, all our other friendships will be even better.

Why is this true? Because this is the way God designed us to function. Remember Matthew 22:37-39?

> *Jesus replied: "Love the Lord your God with all your heart and with all your soul and with all your mind." This is the first and greatest commandment. And the second is like it: "Love your neighbor as yourself."*

God Wants You for His Friend.

We start out as God's enemies. Would you want the perpetrators of the September 11, 2001 attack on the United States for your best friends? Would you welcome these terrorists into your life knowing their heart was full of hatred for you? Would you invite them to go on vacation with you, knowing their desire was to slaughter you, take over your home, and install their friends as rulers over your children?

When we were God's enemies, God planned to make us His friends. While we were still sinners, Christ died for us. In his book, *Caught Off Guard*, William Smith says this:

> ... We humans bring sin, rebellion, death, and separation to the [friendship] equation. But God brings forgiveness, reconciliation, life, and restoration. He brings grace that makes friends of his enemies. ...

> God is not merely kind to people who don't deserve it. He does more than simply help me when I'm struggling and then send me on my way. Instead he pursues me to [build a] relationship—the most precious and beautiful thing in the universe—and to defeat my destructive rebellion. ... Our God keeps pursuing us for relationship, doing what must be done to ensure that it happens.

> ... Do you believe it? Do you believe that God wants to be your friend? Perhaps you believe that God searches diligently for you. You can even muster up the faith to believe that he's doing so for your good. But when you think about all the glorious creatures in the universe and all the truly interesting people who have something to offer, you can't quite believe that God thinks you're especially worth knowing. ...

> You wouldn't be the first to believe those lies. They're the same ones Satan has told for years: that God doesn't truly love his children or really want to know them. There's just enough reasonableness in those thoughts to make them plausible. On one level, it is crazy to believe that the Creator would want anything to do with you or me. I mean, what's in it for him? But it is God himself who says that he wants us, and he backs his words with his actions. ...

> Now it's your turn. ... Do you want the friendship with him that he desires?[52]

---

[52] Smith, William, *Caught Off Guard* (Greensboro, NC: New Growth Press, 2006), p. 22.

Do You Want God as Your Best Friend?

Remember being in grade school and choosing teams? Two team captains were selected, and they got to take turns choosing whom they wanted on their team. Many of us have horrible memories of those occasions. We stood waiting to be selected; desperately wishing our name would be called. We knew we couldn't kick the side of a barn, let alone a kickball, but nevertheless, we desperately wished we would be selected for the recess team. But without athletic skill, many of us were left waiting. No team wanted us.

God wants us on His team. We haven't been left desperately wishing we would be picked. God picked us!

But now let's say, you get to do the choosing. You're the team captain, and you get to make the first selection. Who will be first? Is it going to be Stephanie (because you can control her)? Will it be Tausha (because she won't confront you)? Will it be Crystal (because Crystal is so much fun to be around, you always laugh when you're with her)? Will it be Vera (because she is so prominent in the community)?

The choosing starts when you decide whether you're going to let Christ be your Savior and Lord. You can reject Him. You don't have to have Him on your team. It seems counterintuitive to reject Him after He laid down His life for you but the fact is, you get to choose. Clearly, this is the most important team you'll ever captain, and choosing Christ is the best choice you'll ever make.

This is not a once-in-a-lifetime grade school opportunity, however. Choosing continues with choices to *remain* (John 15:9) in God's love by obeying His commands.

Some of us may have decided we want to choose God for the "escape from hell" team, but when we get to choose for the "popularity" team, we want someone else on the team first. When we get to choose for the "what-to-do-on-Friday" team, we want someone else on the team first. When we get to choose for the "spending money" team, we want someone else on the team first. (In fact, sometimes we don't even want God on those teams.)

Do you want God as your best friend? Do you want God to be your Lord? If you want sweet and precious friendships, you need to make sure you choose the right best friend! Remember what C. S. Lewis said,

> When I have learnt to love God better than my earthly [best friends], I shall love my earthly [best friends] better than I do now. In so far as I learn to love my earthly [best friends] at the expense of God and instead of God, I shall be moving towards the state in which I shall not love my earthly [best friends] at all. When first things are put first, second things are not suppressed but increased.[53]

Authentic Friendship is Based on What You Give; Not on What you Get

One morning while my husband Jeff and I were making the bed, the blanket was hanging way down on my side, so I suggested that Jeff pull the blanket his way. Jeff jokingly asked me, "How come you keep stealing the blanket from me?" To which I replied with tongue-in-cheek, "Honey, I know how hot you get; I was just trying to serve you by taking the blanket."

Make sure that what you call friendship isn't simply selfishness dressed up in pretty language! You see, authentic friendship genuinely puts the needs of others first. This is what God did for us. Our greatest need was to be rescued from the penalty of sin. Praise be to God that in Christ we have redemption through His blood, the forgiveness of sins. God has lavished His love on us!

God's friendship with us is not based on getting something from us, the basis of God's friendship is giving. Genuine friendship is not to be based on what you get, genuine friendship means giving to meet the needs of another.

I think this is particularly illustrated in Matthew 26:50. In this verse we hear Jesus saying, *"Friend, do what you came for."* Do you know to whom Jesus was speaking? Jesus was speaking to Judas. Judas, who was at that moment betraying Christ. As soon as those words were out of Christ's mouth, the men with Judas stepped forward, seized Jesus and arrested him.

---

[53] Lewis, *Letters*, p. 248.

Why would you call a rascal like Judas "friend"? Surely, if anyone should be on Christ's enemy list, it should be Judas. But for Christ, friendship was never about what others could or would do for Him—it was and is about showing love.

Our friendships with others should follow the pattern of Christ. The basis of our friendships should not be what we get; the guiding tenant in our friendships should be what we can give. The foundation of our friendships should not be getting approval, having control, being safe, being right, having fun, being comfortable, or being important. Friendship should be about lavishing love on others in accordance with the riches of God's grace lavished on us.

Our friendships must be shaped not by what we want to get from the relationship but by what God designed.

What next?

Every friendship orientation we've discussed so far is inauthentic. Each friendship orientation discussed to this point has focused on what could be gained from the friendship—acceptance, control, protection, conformity to the rules, pleasure, comfort, or prestige.

Now let's go back through each of our friendship orientations and think about what they would look like if we replaced them with authentic and genuine friendships.

- First, we'll consider what a person *seeks and wants* in genuine friendships.

- Then, we'll consider the *acceptable costs* for a genuine friendship.

- In place of fears and nightmares, we'll consider the *delights and joys* of genuine friends.

- Next, we'll study genuine friendships *seen in action*.

- Finally, we'll examine the *experience of others* in genuine friendships.

Are you ready?

Chapter 12
From Approval-Oriented to Genuine and Authentic Friendships

Holding a homemade "Free Compliments" sign, two Purdue University students received national attention last year for standing along a central walkway on the university's campus and shouting out compliments. Every Wednesday throughout the academic year, rain or shine, snow or humidity, these two young men graced the campus corridor. Passers-by were complimented on their bikes, their hair, their smiles, their hustle, their hard work, their nutritious choice of snacks, their school spirit, and more.

Questioned about standing out in the Indiana weather with no motive other than to give compliments, the guys stated, "I think we brighten the day for a lot of people and that makes people happier." From the smiles, thumbs up, and good will of the Purdue community this would certainly appear to be the case. Not focused on *getting approval*, the "Compliment Guys" showed the character of genuine friends by *giving approval*.

Heart's Desire

In chapter 4, we followed Sophie through a typical day. Sophie yearned for the approval of her friends. For the Sophie's of this world, replacing the desire for approval from people with a desire for God's approval brings freedom and paves the way for genuine and authentic friendships. Having God's approval is the heart's desire of any approval-oriented friend who learns to be a genuine friend.

The phone system in our office also serves as an intercom, giving us the ability to broadcast announcements to the entire building. You may have something similar where you work. Envision having the chief executive officer of your company broadcast an announcement over the intercom that you are a cherished employee and he is well pleased with your work. Not only do all your colleagues hear it, but everyone waiting in the lobby and any service providers in the building hear the announcement too.

God broadcast such an announcement about His Son. God's voice boomed out from heaven announcing, *"This is my Son, whom I love; with him I am well pleased"* (Matthew 3:17). Christ clearly enjoyed the approval of God the Father. Genuine friends long to be like their brother Christ with whom the Father is well pleased. They yearn for God's approval.

When my son, Matt, was learning to clean bathrooms while he was growing up, he once used the brush I keep for cleaning the sinks as a toilet brush. Matt got the toilet really clean, but I never wanted to use the brush on the sinks again. Yuk! The brush's intended use had been twisted and perverted.

When approval-oriented friends like Sophie become authentic friends, they come to realize that their former desire for approval from people was twisted and perverted by sin. As authentic friends there is still a desire for approval, but the desire has been restored to its proper place. The desire now is for the approval of God. Sophie, and those like her, begin to comprehend that if, as a result of pleasing God, others are pleased with them, that's great—bring it on. However, their joy is not dependent on others' approval; their joy comes from pleasing God.

As a genuine friend, Sophie is able to appreciate that pleasing God will frequently result in people being pleased with her as well. She has learned this from the following passages: *"When a man's ways are pleasing to the LORD, he makes even his enemies live at peace with him"* (Proverbs 16:7), and *"Who is going to harm you if you are eager to do good?"* (1 Peter 3:13). Serving God well and seeking to please Him often results in others being pleased with us.

However, Sophie balances this with the truth that if the world hated Christ, the world will hate His followers as well. She is well aware of Christ's teaching in John 15:18-21, where Christ said:

> *If the world hates you, keep in mind that it hated me first. If you belonged to the world, it would love you as its own. As it is, you do not belong to the world, but I have chosen you out of the world. That is why the world hates you. Remember the words I spoke to you: "No servant is greater than his master." If they persecuted me, they will persecute you also. If they obeyed my teaching, they will obey yours also. They will treat you this way because of my name, for they do not know the One who sent me.*

Amazingly, instead of fearing the truths taught in the passage above, Sophie is now able to rejoice and live confidently because she knows that if she is hated by others for pleasing her Savior, God has prepared a great reward for her in heaven.[54] She has concluded that if God blesses her with the approval of others, she will thank God. On the other hand, if following God results in the displeasure of others, she will thank God that she has been worthy of suffering in His name (Acts 5:41). Sophie's most important friend is God.

As a genuine friend, not only does Sophie now treasure God's approval above all else, she desires to give approval. In the past, she often gave approval in a flattering, insincere way. Now Sophie strives to give approval in an edifying way that will encourage others to seek God's approval. She looks for things that are excellent to commend in her friends.

If Sophie could broadcast approval and encouragement all day long, nothing could make her happier. She loves to express her delight in seeing her friends do things God's way. Sophie's compliments have become less focused on externals and more focused on godly character. Instead of tending to give compliments like "I love your dress," you will more frequently hear comments like "You've got a real gift for helping new people feel welcome," or "It helps me persevere when I watch how you handle trials." (The genuine friend may also compliment her friends on

---

[54] Matthew 5:11-12 11: Blessed are you when people insult you, persecute you and falsely say all kinds of evil against you because of me. Rejoice and be glad, because great is your reward in heaven, for in the same way they persecuted the prophets who were before you.

externals, because she recognizes that good taste in clothing, beautiful hair, or a nice home are good gifts from God, and she can rejoice with others in the way God has lavished good things on His creation.)

Acceptable Cost

As a genuine friend, Sophie has learned to be willing to lose man's approval in order to gain God's approval. She cherishes the exhortation found in Galatians 1:10:

> *Am I now trying to win the approval of men, or of God? Or am I trying to please men? If I were still trying to please men, I would not be a servant of Christ.*

Sophie has taught herself to be on guard against trying to win the approval of men by repeatedly asking herself, "Whom am I trying to please?" She wants to be vigilant to make sure she doesn't slip back into her old ways. She longs to be a servant of Christ, who brings joy to her Master.

Whereas in the past Sophie fled from confrontation, as a genuine friend she is now willing to lose man's approval by confronting others. Sophie wants to share the pleasure of God's approval and thus is willing to lovingly approach her friends when she sees areas in their lives which would displease the Father. She is sustained in this by the thought that wise men will love her for confronting them; it is those who are foolish who will respond poorly (Proverbs 9:8; 17:10).

Delight/Joy

The greatest delight and joy of the genuine friend is God's approval. Not only does she want God to be pleased with her, the genuine friend wants to encourage others in their growth in Christlikeness so that they too would please God and someday hear, "Well done, good and faithful servant."

As a genuine friend, Sophie's fear of man has become a fear of disappointing the One who loved her and gave His life for her. She has made it her goal to please Him. Like Paul, in Second Corinthians, chapter five, Sophie is very concerned about others (vs. 11), because she knows what it is like to fear the Lord. As an authentic, genuine friend, she wants to persuade others to make pleasing God as their ambition (vs. 9). No longer does she refrain from letting others know what she believes; she is compelled by the love of Christ (vs. 14) to encourage others to live not for themselves, but for the Savior who died and was raised again (vs. 15). Rather than waiting to learn the opinions of others, Sophie sees herself as an ambassador (vs. 20) with an appeal to make.

Sophie has learned to love God with all her heart, mind and strength, and to love others as herself!

Seen in Action

As an approval-oriented friend, Sophie worried continuously about what others would think of her. Now, as a genuine friend, this godly woman appears confident and peaceful. These attributes have taken root in Sophie's life as she has learned to trust in God. Sophie loves having God as her best friend and regularly studies His word to learn what He would approve and how to grow in her service to Him. Sophie has made God's word her standard.

Trusting in God has helped Sophie learn to be eager to solve problems when they arise in friendships. From Ephesians 4:26-27 Sophie knows that problems not solved quickly give a foothold to Satan. *"In your anger do not sin: Do not let the sun go down while you are still angry, and do not give the devil a foothold."*

Now Sophie is willing to lovingly address issues. Before going to someone to address a problem, Sophie reviews a mental checklist similar to this:

- Have I remembered that God has allowed this problem to help me become more like Christ? (Romans 8:28-29).

- Have I looked for the log in my own eye? Have I examined myself to see where I may be at fault? (Matthew 7:3-5).

- Is my motive in addressing this problem to please God and help my friend? (2 Corinthians 5:9).

- Have I planned the best way to communicate? (Proverbs 14:22).

- Am I prepared to persevere even if this doesn't go as well as I would like? (James 1:2-4).

Once Sophie has thoughtfully planned her words and prayed for God's help, she goes to her friend and communicates. Using her mental checklist has helped Sophie understand what she could have done when her co-worker, Amanda, asked her to lie to their boss. At the time, Sophie handled the problem by pretending she didn't get Amanda's text asking her to tell their boss Amanda was sick. Sophie knows it would not have pleased God to have lied to her boss. Now she also knows that it doesn't please her best friend, God, to ignore problems either.

Sophie decided she could have said something to Amanda like the following.

"In the past, I haven't been a very good friend to you because I was so concerned about getting your approval that I'd basically do anything to get it. I've come to see how unloving and wrong I was to treat you like that. Will you forgive me?

"Amanda, I'll be happy to let our boss know that you won't be at work today. However, if she asks me why you won't be in I'm going to ask her to speak to you personally. I now want to be a friend you can trust, and I really don't believe I can be that kind of friend if I'm not honest. If I lie to our boss, not only could you not be sure that I'd never lie to you, I would know that I was guilty of being a hypocrite—professing to follow God but not obeying Him. Would you still like me to tell our boss you'll be gone today, or would you prefer to talk to her yourself?"

Sophie's mentor, Mrs. Phillips, helped her take steps of growth in overcoming her reluctance to express an opinion or preference. First, Mrs. Phillips helped Sophie understand that to glorify God; Sophie needs to share God's position on clear cut biblical issues.

As an example of this, Mrs. Phillips asked Sophie what position she should take if one of her friends asked if she thought it was okay to have sex with her boyfriend once they were engaged. Sophie responded that she should explain that she believes sex was created by God to be enjoyed only within marriage. "Exactly," exclaimed Mrs. Phillips. "In order to please God, you should adopt God's opinions on clear-cut biblical issues."

While Sophie understood this, she had a harder time knowing what to do in areas where God has given us choices in pleasing Him, such as what restaurant to pick for lunch with her friends.

Mrs. Phillips taught Sophie that she should always start with the motives of her heart when she tries to figure out what to do in such situations. Mrs. Phillips gave Sophie a couple of questions to help her with this.

    a.   Is the reason I want others to choose where to go for lunch because I don't want to lose my friends' approval if I choose a place they don't want to go?

    b.   Do I want others to choose where to go because I think I would be putting their interests first if I allowed them to choose?

If Sophie answers yes to question 'a', she should ask for God's help not to be ruled by a desire for the approval of others. If Sophie answers yes to question 'b', she needs to think through the interests of her friends and guard against making faulty assumptions.

Sophie had never before done anything like this. When Mrs. Phillips asked her to evaluate the interests of her friends when deciding where to eat, the only thing Sophie could come up with was that her friends would want to eat at a place they liked.

Mrs. Phillips cautioned Sophie that her friends probably had several other interests. With Mrs. Phillips' help, they listed some other interests of Sophie's friends.

- To have a decision made quickly and efficiently, so that they don't waste their lunch hour standing around making a decision.

- To go where it won't blow their budget.

- To go where it's quiet enough to talk and be able to hear each other.

- To go where they can all sit together.

- To go where they can get lunch in a timely way and return to work without being late.

- To have someone else share the load of making decisions about where to go.

- To become more like Christ.

- To please God by putting the interests of others first.

"Sophie," Mrs. Phillips said gently, "when you assume your friends will be upset if you choose a place they don't like, you are assuming they are selfish. Like all of us, they may struggle with selfishness, but your job as a loving, genuine friend is to believe that they want to be unselfish. You should not believe they are being selfish unless you have clear, indisputable evidence of selfishness. Now, let's go back to deciding where to go to lunch. Based on the interests we listed, if you put your friends' interests first, what are some places you shouldn't choose?"

Sophie listed several places that were either too slow, too expensive, too far away, too loud, or too crowded. "That still leaves a lot of places to eat," commented Mrs. Philips. "Now you should choose one."

"But what if I really don't have a preference? What if I don't care where we eat?" Sophie asked.

"You are making a faulty assumption if you believe you must have a definite preference in order to make a choice. You can make a choice even if you don't have a preference. You just need to decide," replied Mrs. Phillips.

"Wow, that is really different than what I've done in the past," said a stunned Sophie.

"Practice on me. What will you say to Chastity, Greta, and Holly next time it's your turn to choose?"

Sophie hesitated then said, "Why don't we go to Wendy's, unless someone really wants to go somewhere else.

"Is it okay for me to say that last part, 'unless someone really wants to go somewhere else'?" Sophie probed.

Mrs. Phillips smiled. "Sure," she replied. "Now, tell me how you put the interests of others first by deciding on Wendy's." As Sophie answered her question, Mrs. Phillips quietly rejoiced in the way Sophie has grown in loving God and loving others.

Another of the areas affected by having God as her best friend is Sophie's schedule. As an approval-oriented friend, Sophie frequently overcommitted because she didn't want to say no and lose someone's approval. Even though she continues to be a hard worker, she no longer over-commits. Genuine friends understand that God has entrusted them with responsibilities in many areas, and it would be sinful to regularly neglect God-given responsibilities in order to please others by committing to new responsibilities. While genuine friends are very willing to give up their flexible time to minister to others, they don't routinely sacrifice exercise, prayer, Bible study, sleep, or other obligations in order to make others happy.

What Others Experience

You will probably notice changes in your relationship if you have an approval-oriented friend who becomes a genuine friend. She will likely encourage and exhort you to be like Christ. As an approval-oriented friend, she was very sensitive to any signs which might indicate disapproval. She has now learned to use that sensitivity to minister to you. She notices when you take small steps of growth and commends you. She also notices when you may be discouraged and helps share your load. Having the friendship of this authentic friend would mean you regularly receive expressions of approval and praise.

As her friend, Chastity has noticed changes in Sophie as Sophie has grown to be an authentic, genuine friend. Chastity can see that Sophie has learned to desire God with all her heart, mind and soul, and to love others as herself. Along the way, Chastity has been refreshed, encouraged, loved, and edified. Their friendship has grown to where they can easily talk about the changes Sophie has made.

"Do you remember how you would always ask me, 'Are you upset with me?'" Chastity said to Sophie at lunch one day. "Even if I wasn't upset with you, having you ask me all the time made me upset. I felt as if I had to walk on eggshells around you and say things just right or you would think I was angry. I'm so glad you're not like that anymore. What happened?"

"When I decided to get serious about being God's friend it didn't take too long until I was studying 1 Corinthians 13—the love chapter. One of the principles I learned from that chapter is that love believes the best of others—it trusts. Believing the best was foreign to me. I couldn't remember ever believing the best; I always assumed the worst. I assumed that you (and everyone else) were either already upset with me or could easily be upset with me. I wanted to do whatever it took to make you like me.

"After studying 1 Corinthians 13, I came to understand that if I believed the best about you I needed to believe you would talk to me if you had a problem with me; I should not rely on my feelings and assume you were mad at me. Prior to that, I was guilty of treating you as if you didn't love God or want to obey His word. I was guilty of treating you as if you didn't love me enough to talk to me about problems in order to help me. Basically, I assumed you were just like me—you really only cared about yourself.

"One of the really precious things that happened as I was working on believing the best was that God became my best friend more than ever. I would have these conversations with Him (well, really, I did all the talking) where I would say something to Him like, 'God, this is so hard! It's really hard to believe that she [whoever] isn't upset with me when she hasn't smiled at me since I came in. She's spent all her time talking to that new person. But You've said that love believes the best and that You won't give me more than I can handle, so I'm going to believe she isn't upset with me, she's just trying to get to know that new person and help her feel welcome.'"

"So, do you ever ask anymore if someone is upset with you?" Chastity questioned.

"Only if there are a lot of changes that don't make sense," Sophie replied. "If I see negative changes in our relationship that continue over a period of time I might tell that person what changes I've noticed and ask her to help me understand what to think about what I've observed."

"So what do you do if she doesn't have any explanation for the changes and insists nothing is wrong?" asked Chastity.

"Then I remind myself that I have to believe the best. Believing the best means I need to believe my friend has told me the truth. I've learned that if my friend is lying, God can either reveal the necessary facts so that I can talk with her about it, or God can work in her life to convict her and help her come to me about the problem."

"I've noticed that you don't seem to be afraid of correction anymore," commented Chastity. "In fact, it's been my observation that if anyone has occasion to give correction, instruction, or counsel to you, you make her feel like she has really done you a favor. I haven't seen you respond defensively or apologize profusely in a long time."

Sophie responded, "God has helped me look at correction in a new way. Because I've struggled with talking to people about problems, I realize that it can be really hard to talk to someone when you see something that needs to be addressed. So, when someone loves me enough to get past her fear and talk to me, I'm really thankful she cares enough about me to not let me keep doing things wrong. If people are brave enough to tell me where I'm blowing it, I figure they must really love me.

"Of course, I realize that every once in a while you come across what Proverbs calls an 'angry man,' who is just mad about everything. It's never enjoyable to be around someone like that, but I figure it pleases God if I mine the criticism for gold."

"'Mine criticism for gold?' That's a new one for me. What does that mean?" questioned Chastity.

"It means looking for the nugget of truth in what was said. If I can find that nugget I can still profit from getting chewed out by someone who displays ungodly anger."

"That's helpful," said Chastity. "I've never thought about it that way before."

"Well, it's challenging to apply, but it has helped me grow when I've tried to put it into practice," responded Sophie.

Like Sophie, genuine friends demonstrate a sincere desire to love God with all their heart, mind, soul, and strength and to love others as themselves!

Chapter 13
From Control-Oriented to Genuine
and Authentic Friendships

Heart's Desire

When a control-oriented friend learns to be a genuine friend she longs to be controlled by what God wants. She begins to pray regularly, "Lord help me make your desires my desires." Then she studies God's word to find out what He desires.

In chapter 5, we watched as Victoria sought to control everyone around her. Victoria's heart was ruled by her desire to run the show. She willingly manipulated everyone around her so she could serve her control idol.

For Victoria, and those like her, becoming an authentic, genuine friend requires repenting of their obsession to be in control of every situation. Friends like Victoria demonstrate repentance as they start to cherish passages like Ephesians 5:21:

Submit to one another out of reverence for Christ.

Rather than seeking to dominate others, authentic friends love to put the interests of their friends before their own. As an authentic friend, no longer does Victoria demand control of the TV remote, insist on listening to her music, pout if she has to go to a restaurant she didn't get to choose, or withhold information in order to keep control. As a genuine friend, she asks questions to learn the interests of others because she desires to put their interests ahead of her own.

Acceptable Cost

As a genuine friend, Victoria no longer has to have things done her way. Her husband can set the table without being corrected, her stepson can vacation with his mother without fear of reprisal, and friends can turn down requests without triggering nasty reproaches. Nor does she treat people as if they owe her for serving them. Her attitude reflects the attitude of the servant in Luke 17:7-10. She doesn't see herself as someone who deserves to be thanked. She sees herself as someone who is just doing what she was created to do.[55]

Victoria has learned that being a servant may mean that some people no longer see her as a leader. This is a price she is very willing to pay. Whether others realize it or not, Victoria has come to understand that true leadership is represented by serving. Christ Himself modeled and taught this to His disciples. *"Jesus called them together and said, 'You know that those who are regarded as rulers of the Gentiles lord it over them, and their high officials exercise authority over them. Not so with you. Instead, whoever wants to become great among you must be your servant, and whoever wants to be first must be slave of all'"* (Mark 10:42-44).

As Victoria has studied this passage, she has realized that Christ didn't rebuke His disciples for wanting to be great. Instead, He pointed out to them that they were striving for greatness in the wrong way. Those who want to be great must be servants. Victoria has tried to lord it over people for years, but now that she has repented, she has become a servant.

---

[55] Luke 17:7-10: Suppose one of you had a servant plowing or looking after the sheep. Would he say to the servant when he comes in from the field, "Come along now and sit down to eat"? Would he not rather say, "Prepare my supper, get yourself ready and wait on me while I eat and drink; after that you may eat and drink"? Would he thank the servant because he did what he was told to do? So you also, when you have done everything you were told to do, should say, "We are unworthy servants; we have only done our duty."

Delight/Joy

After she repented of having an idol of control, Victoria wanted to have God as her best friend. She wasn't sure, however, how to show her friendship to God. She longed for a deepening relationship with the Lord, and was ecstatic to read John 15:14: *"You are my friends if you do what I command."* This was exciting! She could grow in her friendship with her Savior by following His commands.

Now Victoria thirsts to know what God says so that she can become a better friend to Him and to others. The descriptions of God's word in Psalm 19 delight her,[56] and Victoria has meditated on them and made them her own:

- God's word is better than a Harvard education, because God's word makes wise the simple (vs. 7).

- God's word is better than your team coming from behind to win the NCAA tournament, because God's word gives joy to the heart (vs. 8).

- God's word is better than night vision goggles when you're camping in the wilderness and hear frightening noises, because God's word gives light to the eyes (vs. 8).

- God's word is better than the Energizer bunny, because God's word endures forever (vs. 9).

- God's word is better than the decision of any Supreme Court judge, because God's word is altogether righteous (vs. 9).

- God's word is better than Jed Clampett striking oil and moving to Beverly Hills, because God's word is more precious than gold (vs. 10).

- God's word is better than a box of Fannie May butter creams, because God's word is sweeter than honey (vs. 10).

- God's word is better than the National Weather Service first alert system, because God's word warns those who study it (vs. 11).

---

[56] Psalm 19:7-11: 7. The law of the LORD is perfect, reviving the soul.
The statutes of the LORD are trustworthy, making wise the simple.
8. The precepts of the LORD are right, giving joy to the heart.
The commands of the LORD are radiant, giving light to the eyes.
9. The fear of the LORD is pure, enduring forever.
The ordinances of the LORD are sure and altogether righteous.
10. They are more precious than gold, than much pure gold; they are sweeter than honey, than honey from the comb.
11. By them is your servant warned; in keeping them there is great reward. (NIV)

- God's word is better than providing information leading to the arrest of a criminal with a reward on his head, because keeping God's word brings great reward (vs. 11).

Victoria has come to delight in serving others and doing things the way her friends like to have them done. She once thought it was stupid to remove her keys from the ignition after she pulled her car into the garage. Now, she puts her keys in her purse, because she knows it pleases her husband not to find them left in the ignition. She used to bristle every time someone asked her to serve or give money. She wanted to help on her terms—when and where she decided. Previously, if friends invited Victoria and Dane to dinner and then asked her to bring a dessert, she grumbled to Dane about people who wanted to have a party but have everyone else do the work and shoulder the expense. Victoria no longer bristles and grumbles. Now she has realized that her time and energy are all gifts from God who expects her to be a good and liberal steward of them.

One of the unexpected delights for Victoria has been the development of "phileo" love for others and from others. Because she isn't striving for control, for the first time she has people in her life who really enjoy being around her. She is able to enjoy the warm affection that used to be missing in her relationships.

Seen in Action

God designed us to have great joy when we give. Everything belongs to God, and as the Creator He is well able to provide anything He wants. Nevertheless, He allows His people to give and be involved in His work. God doesn't hold us at arm's length or make us feel like second class citizens, not worthy or capable of doing His work (even though we're not worthy or capable). God lets us participate in His good plans. We see an example of this when Moses received instruction for constructing the tabernacle. The people had the joy of giving. In fact, they gave so much; they had to be told to stop (Exodus 36).

As a control-oriented friend, Victoria never wanted others to have the upper hand. Therefore, if anyone did anything for her, Victoria made sure she paid back over and above what she had received. (Remember the elaborate dinner she prepared after being invited for dessert at her friends' home.) Victoria has had to train herself to understand that she is serving others when she allows them to give. As an authentic friend, she has learned the grace of receiving and graciously accepting the service of others.

Victoria has also learned that allowing others to give to her creates more intimate relationships. Friends aren't held at arm's length; they are welcomed as co-laborers. When, in pride, she is tempted to refuse help from others, she goes through the following mental self-evaluation checklist:

Do I dislike receiving from others because ...

- People might think I'm needy? (The truth is that I *am* needy. Apart from God I can do nothing.)

- I'm proud or I'm afraid others will think I'm weak? (Again, apart from God I can do nothing.)

- I think they can't afford to give? (Yet God especially blesses them for giving out of their poverty.)

- I want to hold them at arm's length? By allowing them to give to me I am no longer able to distance myself from them like an impersonal benevolent benefactress. (God allows me to give to Him. He allows me to be His ambassador. He doesn't treat me like a second class citizen.)

- It makes me feel that I am obligated to them, and I want them to be obligated to me?

- I don't care about helping them grow or increasing their joy? (Acts 20:35 says it's better to give than receive. By refusing to let them give to me, I'm refusing to let them have the joy of giving.)

- I've forgotten that everything belongs to God? (When God entrusts me with a gift from someone, He wants me to make use of it for His purposes. I should use what others give me to serve God and others.)

Like Sophie in our previous chapter, Victoria benefitted from the teaching of a mentor once she repented. One of the areas in which Victoria needed help was learning to allow others to do things their way when she thought her way was superior. As a bright and competent young woman, Victoria was often able to come up with the most effective and efficient plans for getting things done. When she began to submit to others, she struggled when their plans weren't as good as hers.

Victoria's mentor, Mrs. Jamison, encouraged Victoria to change by learning to distinguish what is good, what is better, and what is best. Mrs. Jamison used driving across town to help illustrate her point:

"What road would you take to get from here to the south side of town?" asked Mrs. Jamison.

"I'd take Creasy, it's the shortest," Victoria replied.

"What if I was driving and I took Montgomery?" asked Mrs. Jamison.

"I'd probably tell you Creasy is shorter," said Victoria.

"In other words, my way is good (it will get me to the south side) but your way is better," summarized Mrs. Jamison.

"Correct," said Victoria.

"What is the *best* way?" asked Mrs. Jamison with a smile.

"Creasy," responded Victoria.

"No, Creasy was the "better" way, it's not the *best* way," countered Mrs. Jamison.

"It's not? I can't think of a road that's faster than Creasy," said Victoria.

"The *best* way is the way that allows you to bring the most glory and honor to God. Therefore, the best way is to put the interests of others first," explained Mrs. Jamison. "Your way is a good route, but God isn't as concerned about you taking the shortest route as you are. He's concerned about you loving Him with all your heart, mind, and soul, and loving others as yourself.

"Think through this with me. Is there anything sinful about driving down either Creasy or Montgomery?" questioned Mrs. Jamison.

"No."

"Then if you want to put the interests of others first, and I want to take Montgomery, what's the *best* route for you when you're riding with me?" asked Mrs. Jamison.

"I think it would be Montgomery. Is that right?" Victoria responded.

"Yes, can you tell me why?" asked Mrs. Jamison.

"Because taking Montgomery allows me to put your interests first," answered Victoria.

"Right, and Victoria, it's not sinful to explain to others why your route is better, but you may find it difficult to do that with a pure heart for a while. Do you know what I mean by that?"

"I do know," said Victoria. "I'm so used to bossing people around and expecting others to do things my way that I doubt I could explain how my way is better without a) telling people the road I'd take out of a desire, not to be helpful, but to get it done my way or b) sounding like I was still being bossy."

"I agree," said Mrs. Jamison. "For a while, you may find it best not to offer advice unless you're asked. This will give you a chance to grow."

The first time Victoria tried to apply these principles she chaffed at how inefficient it was to follow the way of her friends. After chatting with Mrs. Jamison about her struggle, they came up with a strategy to help her. In such situations, every time Victoria wanted to take charge, she was to use that as her reminder to thank God for the opportunity to grow in putting off control as her idol and for putting on loving God as her supreme desire. With practice, Victoria became more and more thankful.

What Others Experience

One Saturday morning as they were walking, Victoria's walking partner, Debra, thanked Victoria for slowing down to her pace. "I know you could go lots faster without me. Thanks for scaling back to my speed," Debra said.

Victoria responded, "I might be able to go a little bit faster than you, but you've gotten so much faster I don't think it will be long before I'm not going to be able to keep up with you. I don't think you realize how much faster you've become. I'm afraid you're going to want to start jogging pretty soon and then I'll never be able to keep up."

Debra replied, "I can't see jogging ever happening, especially if it meant I couldn't have you as my partner. You know, you used to intimidate me, but over the past several months, I feel like we've grown lots closer."

"It seems that way to me too," said Victoria. "I've noticed that as I've worked on not being in control, most of my friendships have gotten better. I never knew friendships could be close. In the past I was always trying to get other people to do what I thought was best for them. I was so blinded by my desire for control that I talked myself into believing my control was for their good."

Debra responded, "Because it seemed as if you always knew best, it was easiest for me to let you make all the decisions. I didn't have to think or take responsibility for anything, because you had it all figured out. While that was enjoyable to some extent, it probably didn't help me grow. It's kind of like always riding a bike with training wheels on it.

"When I was with you, I often felt like you were wearing one of those T-shirts that said, 'I'm with stupid.' The finger on that T-shirt always pointed to me. It's not like that anymore. Now you encourage me to figure out the best way to do things, and I'm really starting to enjoy the challenge. That's especially true since I know you won't make me feel ignorant if I don't always figure it out right," admitted Debra.

By this time, tears were streaming down Victoria's face. "Oh Debra, please forgive me. I *have* treated you like you were stupid. I'm so sorry! Will you forgive me?"

"Of course, I will forgive you, my precious friend. I love you!" was Debra's reply.

Later that afternoon, Victoria got ready to mow the lawn for her elderly neighbor, Mrs. Princhett. When Mrs. Princhett's husband died in March, Victoria began mowing her yard since Mrs. Princhett's children all lived in other states. Frequently when she finished mowing, she and Mrs. Princhett would sit on the front porch with a glass of lemonade and chat while Victoria cooled off. A warm friendship was developing between them.

Today, before Victoria began mowing, Mrs. Princhett asked her to step into the garage with her. In the garage was a new riding lawn mower, with a big pink bow on it. "Victoria," said Mrs. Princhett, "I wanted to say thank you for mowing my grass for me. Before my husband died, I never concerned myself with cutting the grass. He loved to keep the lawn looking good, and I just let him do it. I had never mowed the grass in my life.

"The first time you mowed for me, I sat inside and cried. God had taken care of my need in an unexpected way, and I was overwhelmed by His goodness. You've been such a blessing to me.

"Because God has blessed me, I wanted to bless you as well. I'd like for you and Dane to have this new riding mower."

Victoria flung her arms around Mrs. Princhett and kissed her cheek. "I don't know what to say," she exclaimed. "Your generosity has left me speechless. Thank you so much! I might just start mowing the lawns for everyone in the neighborhood!"

Later, Victoria told her husband that she'd had to bite her tongue to keep from blurting out to Mrs. Princhett, "You shouldn't have done that. This is too much. I can't accept it from you."

Victoria told Dane, "I think Mrs. Princhett would have been hurt if she'd gone to all that trouble and sacrifice, and then I refused to accept her gift. Now that we have this new mower I was wondering what you would think of taking some of the money we've been saving for a new one and giving it to the food pantry."

"Sure," replied Dane. "And what about using some of it to buy fertilizer for Mrs. Princhett's yard? Then you can bless her more often!" he said as he winked at Victoria.

Victoria took the pink bow off the lawn mower and put it on the door of her bedroom closet. The bow served as a visible reminder to Victoria of the joy of learning to love God with all your heart, mind, soul, and strength, and to love others as yourself.

Chapter 14
From Protection-Oriented to Genuine and Authentic Friendships

If you have read the books *Dorie,* or *No Place to Cry,* by Dorie Van Stone, you know that if anyone ever had a reason to be "protection-oriented" in their friendships, it was Dorie. Dorie was forsaken by her parents and dumped into a wicked foster home. In that home, she was permitted to take only one bath a month and wash her hair every eight weeks.

Dorie writes, "My hair became matted, and I developed head lice, so my head was shaved. To hide my embarrassment, I went to school with my head wrapped in a towel. The other children would pull it off and laugh, calling me cruel names. Dirt encased itself around my wrists and ankles. When I walked into the classroom, I'd hear the other students say, 'There's Stinky!' as they turned their backs toward me."[57]

These experiences were not the worst of her trials, yet her suffering didn't have the power to cause Dorie to become protection-oriented in her relationships. In *No Place to Cry,* Dorie writes,

---

[57] Van Stone, Doris, *No Place to Cry: The Hurt and Healing of Sexual Abuse* (Chicago: Moody Press, 1990), p. 26-27.

"Don't believe the psychiatrists who state that experiences of abuse will ruin you for the rest of your life and that you will never be normal. Unfortunately, many people have believed the lie that past abuse will ruin all your chances for happiness. Not so. When Christ promised that our joy would be full, I believe He meant it for all Christians, regardless of their backgrounds. He is indeed able to heal the broken-hearted. For example, I had the good fortune to be married to an understanding husband who loved me despite my abuse. He was tender and compassionate and through his love our [marriage] was beautiful and fulfilling. That is proof of what God is able to do." [58]

Now, Dorie doesn't say this, but do you think her beautiful and fulfilling marriage would have happened if she had been protection-oriented?

Heart's Desire

As we saw in chapter 6, the goal of the protection-oriented friend is to never let anyone hurt her. This changes as she becomes a genuine friend. Now her desire is to make sure that she doesn't hurt God or others by sinning against them. Because she knows how much sinful choices can hurt, the authentic friend learns to earnestly desire to follow after God's ways so that she will not grieve Him by any sinfulness on her part. She longs to be growing in personal righteousness and holiness. The genuine friend also yearns to protect her friends from the devastating effects of sin by encouraging them in their obedience to God and growth in the likeness of Christ.

In chapter 6, we saw how Emily was enslaved to her desire to be safe. She lived her life looking for relationships in which she wouldn't get hurt. She was always on the alert for signs that a friend would hurt her and she regularly ended relationships she believed were getting too intimate and thus made her vulnerable. For Emily and those like her, their slavish devotion to safety is their idol. To be a genuine and authentic friend, a protection-oriented friend needs to repent and learn to trust God and love others.

---

[58] Ibid, p. 29.

Emily has been stunned to learn that God is able to use everything for her good and His glory. She loves God's promise in Romans 8:28, that God works all things together for good for the believer—even hurtful things.

> *And we know that in all things God works for the good of those who love him, who have been called according to his purpose.*

From verse 29, Emily has come to understand that the good that God is working in her life is to make her like His Son.

> *For those God foreknew he also predestined to be conformed to the likeness of his Son, that he might be the firstborn among many brothers.*

Being like Christ has become Emily's highest goal. As Emily has pondered God's goodness, she finds herself marveling as Paul did in Romans 8:31:

> *What, then, shall we say in response to this? If God is for us, who can be against us?*

And Emily finds Romans 8:32 a compelling reason to trust God:

> *He who did not spare his own Son, but gave him up for us all—how will he not also, along with him, graciously give us all things?*

Finally, Emily is comforted in the knowledge that even if she is forsaken by others, she will never be forsaken by God. She clings to His assurance in Roman 8:35-39 that nothing can separate us from His love.

> *Who shall separate us from the love of Christ? Shall trouble or hardship or persecution or famine or nakedness or danger or sword? As it is written: "For your sake we face death all day long; we are considered as sheep to be slaughtered."*
>
> *No, in all these things we are more than conquerors through him who loved us. For I am convinced that neither death nor life, neither angels nor demons, neither the present nor the future, nor any powers, neither height nor depth, nor anything else in all creation, will be able to separate us from the love of God that is in Christ Jesus our Lord.*

Not only is it Emily's desire, and those like her, to trust God, they want to love others. In the past, Emily has selfishly been concerned solely about protecting herself. Now she wants to do what is best for others and protect them from any hurt they would be caused if she were to sin against them.

Emily has posted little notes all over her apartment which say, "Perfect love drives out fear."[59] She wants the reminder that when she begins to focus on her fear of getting hurt, she does not love others. The focus of love is "How can I give to others?" or "How can I serve others?" On the other hand, the focus of fear is "What is going to happen to me?" or "How am I going to be hurt?"

Perfect love is able to drive out fear because it is impossible to focus on "How can I give to others?" and on "How will I be hurt?" at the same time. The two things cannot be done simultaneously, because they are opposites.

Using her Post-it Note reminders, Emily has started to plan ways to show love and to immediately pray for God's blessing on others when her old fears start to return. Emily wants to love God with all her heart, mind, and soul, and to love others as herself.

Acceptable Cost

As a genuine friend, Emily is willing to endure trial if necessary. No longer is she terrified by the thought of being hurt. She has learned that if she must endure a trial, 1) it will only last for a 'little while' (the absolute longest it could last would be until death) and 2) it gives her an opportunity to prove that her best friend is God; that she is a 'genuine friend.'

She is backed up in this belief by 1 Peter 1:6-7.

> *In this you greatly rejoice, though now for a <u>little while</u> you may have had to suffer grief in all kinds of trials. These have come so that your faith—of greater worth than gold, which perishes even though refined by fire—<u>may be proved genuine</u> and may result in praise, glory and honor when Jesus Christ is revealed.*
> (Emphasis added)

In order to be a genuine friend, Emily is now willing to be vulnerable. She has had to work hard on the issue of vulnerability. As a protection-oriented friend, "vulnerability" was a dirty word. Emily hated the thought of opening herself up to the point where others could hurt her, but she has been convicted by Christ's statement to His disciples that no servant is greater than his master. Christ opened Himself up to tremendous hurt by

---

[59] 1 John 4:18.

coming to earth as a man and dying a horrible death on the cross. Emily has taken herself to task for functioning as if it was okay for Christ to be vulnerable for her, but it wasn't okay for her to ever be vulnerable with others.

Delight/Joy

In the past, Emily tried to use her own logic to make sense out of hurtful relationships. When she wasn't able to arrive at a satisfactory reason for undergoing pain in a relationship, she decided her best course of action was to try to protect herself from future hurt. Despite the fact that this course of action wasn't very effective, Emily kept trying.

One of the things that has helped Emily become a genuine friend was to understand that God's ways are not our ways; His ways are higher than our ways (Isaiah 55:8-9). Now, Emily looks forward to seeing how God will use everything for her good and His glory, and she longs to become an oak of righteousness, a planting of the Lord for the display of His splendor, just like the folks to whom Isaiah prophesied (Isaiah 61:3). Nothing could bring her more delight. The picture of becoming a majestic, strong oak, able to weather storms with its branches held high is such a contrast to the cringing, cowardly Emily who ran for cover at the merest hint of a relationship storm that Emily laughs in delight just to think of it.

Seen in Action

When Emily learned that the theme of 1 Peter was suffering, she decided to memorize the whole book. Many things in 1 Peter have encouraged her, and she has put the principles she has learned into practice in her friendships. She regularly reviews what she has memorized with her mentor, Mrs. Mixon.

Emily initially struggled with being open about her failures. She didn't see how openness could help others or glorify God. One day Mrs. Mixon said to her, "Listen to this. I think what William Smith has written in chapter 18 of his book, *Caught Off Guard*, will really encourage you." Mrs. Mixon read:

> Surprising as it may be, [God] so thoroughly redeems us that even our failures can bring him glory and benefit his people. Paul the apostle was very familiar with such radical redemption. Far from being embarrassed by his past,

he regularly dredged it up, publicly discussing his failures.[60]

At first, that seems a little strange. Its one thing to confess your sins at the time you committed them; it's another to keep drawing attention to sins from the past. Why would you want to remind people of how bad you were? If God remembers our sins no more, why does Paul keep them in mind? It seems even stranger given our assumptions about preachers. Aren't preachers like Paul supposed to be positive role models, pointing us to what is right? It almost seems counterproductive for Paul to talk about the ways he had sinned. Can you think of another occupation that emphasizes its past failures?

Suppose you were thumbing through the Yellow Pages and came across a restaurant ad that claimed, "We used to burn food and poison our customers, but that was last year. Come try us now!" How quickly would you grab your phone to make reservations? Or what about a plumber advertising, "I used to break sinks, but I'm a lot better now. Let me come over and work on yours!" Such claims don't inspire much confidence. They're truthful but unlikely to garner much business.

Yet that's what Paul does. He tells you, "I used to persecute the church, but now I preach the gospel." Just like the early Christians in Acts, you're tempted to think, *Not in my church you're not!* Paul takes aspects of his life that seem better left forgotten and regularly puts them on display. Why? When Paul talks about his past, he reminds you that being the "worst of sinners" includes being a blasphemer, a persecutor, and an enemy of Jesus.[61] Yet he says he received mercy so that Christ's patience with him would be an example to others who seek him. Paul says that his public confessions serve two ends: they give glory to God and hope to others.

Just as before and after photos show you the effect of an exercise program, cosmetic surgery, or a weight loss drug, Paul's history shows the effect that Jesus has had in his

---

[60] Acts 22:3-5; Galatians 1:13; Philippians 3:6; 1 Corinthians 15:9; 1 Timothy 1:15-16.
[61] 1 Timothy 1:12-17.

life. He doesn't mind highlighting what he was before Jesus changed him because in so doing he highlights Jesus' glory. You can't miss the brilliant diamonds of God's patience when displayed against the dark velvet of Paul's former life. Far from being a press-hungry celebrity reveling in his degradation, hungry for any and all attention, Paul talks about his past sins because he longs to draw your attention to Jesus.

Confessing his sins also provides hope to other people. If Paul had merely been a nice man when he converted to Christianity, his testimony would not give as much hope to people who had sinned flagrantly. But this way, people who are unsure whether Jesus will receive them can compare themselves with Paul, a deceived, self-righteous, violent murderer who disguised his activities with religious trappings. If Jesus could save Paul, he can do the same for them. Paul's confession inspires others with hope.

Because Paul knows he's accepted by God for Christ's sake, he doesn't need to make himself look better than he is. He can look beyond self-interest and be concerned for a larger world. In this manner, Paul lives out Jesus' two great commandments—love God and love your neighbor—in the way he deals with his past. He demonstrates that you are willing to talk about your failings if your goal is to demonstrate the greatness of God's glory and to help other people.[62]

Emily borrowed the book and read chapter 18 several more times, taking time to digest what she read. The next time Emily and Mrs. Mixon got together, Emily asked Mrs. Mixon to help her figure out how she could use her failures to demonstrate God's greatness.

Mrs. Mixon suggested that she and Emily come up with some questions to help guide her in talking about areas in which she struggled. Together they developed a flow chart that Emily could use as a guide.

---

[62] Smith, William, *Caught Off Guard*, p. 147-148.

Should I Publicly Discuss My Struggles and Failures?

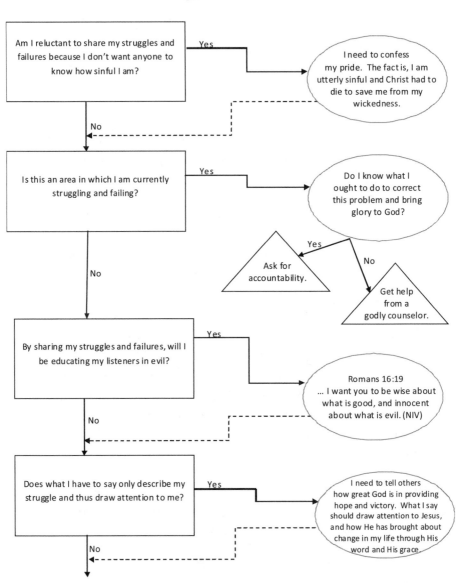

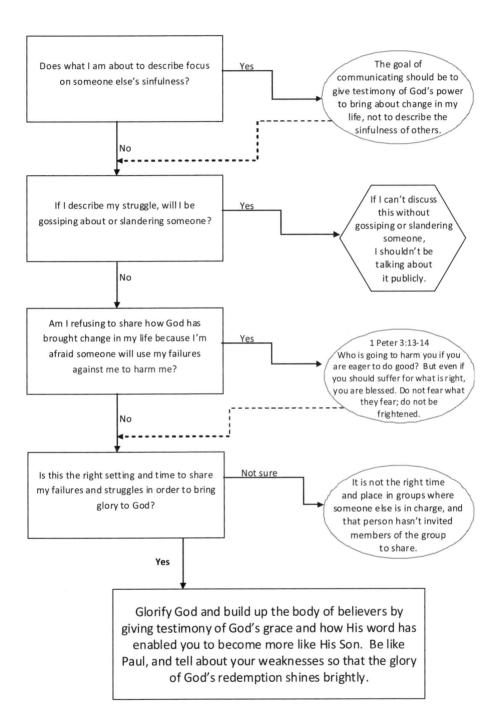

Does what I am about to describe focus on someone else's sinfulness? — Yes → The goal of communicating should be to give testimony of God's power to bring about change in my life, not to describe the sinfulness of others.

No ↓

If I describe my struggle, will I be gossiping about or slandering someone? — Yes → If I can't discuss this without gossiping or slandering someone, I shouldn't be talking about it publicly.

No ↓

Am I refusing to share how God has brought change in my life because I'm afraid someone will use my failures against me to harm me? — Yes → 1 Peter 3:13-14 Who is going to harm you if you are eager to do good? But even if you should suffer for what is right, you are blessed. Do not fear what they fear; do not be frightened.

No ↓

Is this the right setting and time to share my failures and struggles in order to bring glory to God? — Not sure → It is not the right time and place in groups where someone else is in charge, and that person hasn't invited members of the group to share.

Yes ↓

Glorify God and build up the body of believers by giving testimony of God's grace and how His word has enabled you to become more like His Son. Be like Paul, and tell about your weaknesses so that the glory of God's redemption shines brightly.

"Listen to this," Emily requested one day when she and Mrs. Mixon were having a cup of coffee. "I decided to write out a testimony of how God has been at work in my struggles. I'd like to go over it with you to make sure that what I say glorifies God."

"I'd love to hear it," exclaimed Mrs. Mixon.

Emily read, "Early in my life I had some relationships that were very painful. I responded to the pain by becoming very fearful. As time went on, my fear began to rule my life; I made it my goal to never be hurt again. I also became angry and bitter at God, deciding that if He would allow me to experience something as painful as what I had gone through, He couldn't be trusted. I decided the only person I could trust was myself.

"To avoid pain, I had to be constantly vigilant. I didn't care if I hurt other people, as long as I didn't get hurt. I didn't care if I spoke to them unkindly or got sinfully angry. I didn't care if my friends were hurt when I refused to trust them. I didn't care if my friends were hurt when I continuously reminded them of the ways in which they failed in our relationship. All I cared about was that I didn't get hurt.

"If my friends ended our relationship because I was so unpleasant and unloving, I just used that as another reason to be bitter and not to trust anyone. But God was incredibly patient with me. He is God, everything on earth belongs to Him, and at any point He could have said, 'I've had it with you!' That's exactly how I was treating everyone in my life. If they crossed the line I had drawn in my mind I basically said, 'That's it! I've had it with you!' But God didn't treat me as I was treating other people. He continued to love me.

"One day I realized that trusting in myself wasn't bringing me much happiness. It seemed like all around me people had the kind of friendships I wanted, but I repeatedly lost friends or ended relationships. I was living proof of Jeremiah 17:5-6:

> *This is what the LORD says: 'Cursed is the one who trusts in man, who depends on flesh for his strength and whose heart turns away from the LORD. He will be like a bush in the wastelands; he will not see prosperity when it comes. He will dwell in the parched places of the desert, in a salt land where no one lives.'*

"People all around me were experiencing 'prosperity.' They had sweet relationships with others but I was dwelling in a land where no one lives. Trusting in myself was miserable! Then, God mercifully granted me the gift of repentance. Now I know what it's like to experience Jeremiah 17:7-8.

> *But blessed is the man who trusts in the LORD, whose confidence is in him. He will be like a tree planted by the water that sends out its roots by the stream. It does not fear when heat comes; its leaves are always green. It has no worries in a year of drought and never fails to bear fruit.*

"Now that I'm learning to love and serve others, I'm finding endless opportunities. And God is blessing me by allowing me to meet others who also want to love and minister to people. The fellowship with these friends is incredible. I had no idea what I was missing all those years when I was desperately trying not to get hurt. I was willing to settle for simply an absence of pain. Now I can see, at least in part, what God really intended for relationships, and I would never want to go back to my old ways. It's like discovering Lake Tahoe when all I'd ever seen was a mud puddle."

As she grew in authenticity, Emily learned that she had to change the way she thought about pain and hurt. As a protection-oriented friend, Emily was convinced that any and all pain was bad.

"Emily, have you ever heard of Dr. Paul Brand?" asked Mrs. Mixon.

"No, is he a local doctor?" asked Emily.

"No, not local. In fact, he died in 2003. Dr. Paul Brand pioneered the idea that leprosy causes loss of the sensation of pain in areas it affects. Now, wouldn't it be nice not to have to feel pain? Why wouldn't we all wish to have leprosy and never experience pain again?"

"You're setting me up, aren't you?" smiled Emily. "But keep going, I want to hear where you're going with this."

"As a doctor in India in the 1900s, Dr. Brand and his wife encountered 'leprosy beggars.'[63] These were individuals who were deformed, blind, and crippled due to leprosy.

"As he studied leprosy patients, Dr. Brand developed the theory that the horrible results of the disease came about because leprosy patients had lost the sense of pain. The disease was not a flesh-devouring fungus as was commonly believed. Rather, the disease attacked the nerve cells, causing a loss of the sense of pain.[64]

"According to Dr. Brand,

> The gradual loss of pain leads to misuse of those body parts most dependent on pain's protection. A person uses a hammer with a splintery handle, does not feel the pain, and an infection flares up. Another steps off a curb, spraining an ankle, and, oblivious, keeps walking. Another loses use of the nerve that triggers the eyelid to blink every few seconds for lubricating moisture; the eye dries out, and the person becomes blind.[65]"

"I get it, Emily said. "What you're saying is that God ordained pain for our good and protection. Together she and Mrs. Mixon decided to compile a list of ways pain can be a friend. The two women initially listed the following.

Pain can be my friend because:

- I can learn to delight in God's law and learn His decrees (Psalm 119:17).
- Pain gives me an opportunity to develop perseverance (James 1:3).
- Pain gives me an opportunity to show loyalty to God (1 Peter 1:6-7).
- Pain gives me an opportunity to become like Christ (Romans 8:29).
- Perseverance developed in pain leads to maturity (James 1:4).
- Faithfulness in pain leads to reward (James 1:12).
- Pain can prevent me from continuing in sin (Psalm 119:67).
- Pain can prevent me from making sinful choices in the first place (2 Corinthians 12:7).

---

[63] www.tlm-ni.org/Brand.thm From July 10, 2009.
[64] Yancey, Philip and Brand, Paul, *In the Likeness of God* (Grand Rapids, MI, 2004), p. 54.
[65] Ibid, p. 54-55.

- Pain can help me see how awful sin is - it really hurts.
- Pain helps me better understand the price Christ paid in suffering for my sins.
- Pain can help me be sympathetic.
- Pain can prevent me from being proud.
- Pain makes me turn to God for help instead of believing I'm self-sufficient (2 Corinthians 12:9-10).
- Pain gives me an opportunity to be an example for others, to prevent them from sinning and suffering.
- My pain may encourage others to seek salvation (2 Timothy 2:8).
- By enduring pain I can properly reign with God (2 Timothy 2:12).
- By enduring pain I can experience joy at a level I would never have known otherwise. I can rejoice with exultation. (1 Peter 4:13).

What Others Experience

Authentic friends have a balanced view of pain. On the one hand, they never want to cause pain to others by behaving wickedly or sinning against them. On the other hand, they are willing to cause pain for the following righteous reasons:

- To keep their friends from sinning against God.
- To help their friends take steps of growth in Christlikeness.
- To warn their friends that what they are doing is offensive to God.
- To encourage their friends to repent.
- To help their friends understand they are sinners who need Christ as Savior.
- To warn their friends of danger.

Genuine friends don't want to be like the prophets in Jeremiah's time who said, "Peace, peace," when there was no peace. They don't want their friends to believe everything is okay in their lives if it's really not.

"Emily," said Mrs. Mixon after watching Emily struggle with the thought of causing pain, "what's the best thing anyone could ever do for a friend?"

"Probably to lead them to Christ," Emily responded.

"But God's word says that we are all desperately wicked and that in order to come to Christ we have to admit we are sinners. Aren't you afraid that if you tell a friend that she's a sinner, she'll be hurt?"

"Yes, but if she doesn't trust in Christ to save her, she'll be hurt much worse," Emily responded.

"So you wouldn't regret hurting her feelings by telling her she's a sinner?"

"No," said Emily.

"You just came to the same conclusion Paul reached in 2 Corinthians 7 after he hurt his friends by pointing out how they needed to repent and change. He was glad he had confronted them because they grew from it. Hurting his friends was worth creating the pain they experienced, because the pain ultimately helped them."

"Are you familiar with Proverbs 27:6?" Mrs. Mixon asked. "I think it's a verse you'll like."

"Wounds from a friend can be trusted, but an enemy multiplies kisses," read Emily.

"Why could wounds from a friend be trusted?" asked Mrs. Mixon.

"Because you know they love you and want what's best for you," answered Emily, "Just like Paul with the Corinthians."

"What does the last part of the verse mean, 'An enemy multiplies kisses'?" Mrs. Mixon followed up.

"The picture I get is of someone who always tells you what you want to hear, all the while hating your guts," replied Emily. "Like naughty boys trying to lure a cat to them by coaxing, 'Here Kitty, Kitty,' so they can tie cans on its tail."

Emily soon had an opportunity to put these truths into practice with her friend Francesca.

"I found this dress on the clearance rack for 70% off this weekend. I couldn't believe it! Do you like it?" chattered Francesca as they left church together.

Emily paused. "I like the color on you. It really brings out your beautiful eyes. However, I'm not as sure I like the style. You've got a dreamy figure and that dress broadcasts your cleavage to everyone. I'm not sure how much it helps the guys around us think pure thoughts about you," replied Emily gently.

"Yeah, well, okay, see ya," said Francesca abruptly.

Late that afternoon, Emily's phone rang. When she heard Francesca's voice, she got a knot in her stomach.

"Emily," said Francesca after Emily answered, "do you have a minute?"

"Sure," Emily responded nervously.

"I don't think I responded very graciously after we talked about my dress this morning. I wanted to follow-up and thank you for being honest with me. To be frank, I was a little upset at first, mostly because I knew what you said was true, and I didn't really want to hear it. But you were right, and I wanted to thank you for what you said.

"Emily, it's been a long time since I've had a friend who tried to help me be a better person. Because I've heard you talk about ways you've blown it and what God has been teaching you, I knew you weren't just being self-righteous. Even if I don't respond very well at first, I want you to know that I'm really thankful to have a friend like you," Francesca said sincerely.

After chatting a few more minutes they ended the call. Emily immediately got on her knees before God and humbly thanked Him for helping her do right. Emily has become a friend who loves God with all her heart, soul, mind, and strength, and who loves her neighbor as herself.

Chapter 15
From Rightness-Oriented to Genuine and Authentic Friendship

I sometimes watch *Antiques Roadshow* on channel 20 in our local viewing area. As the various participants show off their antique treasures, its fun to guess how much their stuff is worth. I love it when some ugly, dirt-encrusted relic found buried in someone's barn turns out to be worth tens of thousands of dollars.

Disappointingly, not every treasure is worth what the owners believe. Occasionally, some earnest inheritors learn that the heirloom passed down from Great Aunt Millie is worthless. Until this time, the heirs may have had it proudly displayed in their living room. Even if it was ugly, their treasure was accorded a place of honor in their home. But in one sixty minute *Roadshow* the heirloom goes from masterpiece to junk. What was formerly a showpiece goes out with tomorrow's trash as people learn their treasure isn't worth anything.

Heart's Desire

This is exactly the experience of the rightness-oriented friend who becomes genuine and authentic. What she formerly treasured, her rightness and her honor, loses all its value. She now considers it rubbish. The authentic friend has come to understand Paul's declaration in Philippians 3:7-9:

> *But whatever was to my profit I now consider loss for the sake of Christ. What is more, I consider everything a loss compared to the surpassing greatness of knowing Christ Jesus my Lord, for whose sake I have lost all things. I consider them rubbish, that I may gain Christ and be found in him, not having a righteousness of my own that comes from the law, but that which is through faith in Christ—the righteousness that comes from God and is by faith.*

In Philippians 3:4-6, Paul points out his rightness credentials. "You think you're good? I'm better," Paul declares. Then he lists his pedigree. Paul is not just trash–talking, however. Paul's pedigree really is better than any potential competitor. Get the trophy ready, Paul can take on all the competition and crush his opponents.

But you won't find any rightness trophy on the mantle of Paul's living room fireplace. You're more likely to find it by digging through Paul's trash. The trophy Paul wanted to display was an intimate relationship with Christ. He wanted to know Christ. Paul wanted a deep and personal relationship, not a shallow or superficial friendship. Paul's desire for an intimate relationship was so deep that he even wanted to understand Christ's suffering. *"I want to know Christ and the power of his resurrection and the fellowship of sharing in his sufferings, becoming like him in his death, and so, somehow, to attain to the resurrection from the dead"* (Philippians 3:10-11).

Like Paul, when rightness-oriented friends repent, whatever was to their credit they now consider rubbish for the sake of Christ. Their friendship with Christ becomes the most important thing in the world to them. Christ is now the masterpiece prominently displayed in the living rooms of their lives.

For Justine, the rightness-oriented friend we met in chapter 7, what has now become most important in her life is her *relationship* with God. Whereas in the past rules trumped relationship, she now understands that the law is a tool.

First, the law shows us how far we fall short of God's holiness. The law shows us how desperately we need a Savior in order to have a relationship with the One who is perfectly holy and can't look upon sin with favor.

- Just as a mountain of garbage at the dump falls short of the splendor of the Rocky Mountains, the law shows us how far we fall short of God's holiness. Both are mountainous, but no one will ever stand in awe of the majesty of garbage.
- Just as a water treatment plant falls short of Iceland's pristine waters, the law shows us how far we fall short of God's holiness. Both have pure water, but no one would plan a vacation to visit a water treatment plant.
- Just as a sewage pit falls short of the Grand Canyon, the law shows us how far we fall short of God's holiness. You can stand on the edge of both and look into the pit, but you don't send postcards of the sewage pit to the folks back home.

Seeing God's holiness spotlighted by the law illuminates our understanding. It reveals the fake for what it really is. Would you ever admire your rightness after you've seen God's holiness?

Additionally, the law guides us in knowing how to develop a more intimate relationship with God and in knowing how to bring delight to our precious Savior. That's why the psalmist says the law is more precious to him than thousands of pieces of silver and gold (Psalm 119:72).

My husband's favorite pie is Dutch apple. When I want to show love to Jeff, one of the ways I demonstrate my love is by making Dutch apple pie. On the other hand, Jeff doesn't like oatmeal raisin cookies so I don't bake oatmeal raisin cookies for Jeff. Learning what Jeff likes and dislikes helps me do a better job of loving him.

The same principle holds true in our relationship with our best friend, God. God has communicated that He loves it when I am kind, compassionate, and forgiving. Conversely, God hates it when I'm rude, selfish, and greedy. Learning what God likes and dislikes helps me show my love for Him. Just as I can delight Jeff by bringing him a piece of warm Dutch apple pie, we can delight God by practicing kindness, compassion, and forgiveness. This is why the psalmist delights in God's law. This is why the psalmist is consumed with longing to know God's laws (Psalm 119:20).

Justine now desires to promote God's goodness and righteousness, not her own. She now yearns for true holiness in her friendships. She wants to do what is right in the eyes of God. She wants to love God and she wants to love others.

Acceptable Cost

As a rightness-oriented friend, Justine worked hard to appear as if she didn't have any faults. Now, as an authentic friend, Justine is willing to publicly acknowledge her failure in order to promote God's glory. She wants people to be able to look at her and say, "Wow! If God could use someone like her, surely He could use me too! If God would be merciful to her, surely He would also show mercy to me."

Justine has confidence that her failures can encourage others just as Paul was confident that his life could be an encouragement to others. Justine keeps Paul's words in 1 Timothy1:15-16 on her bathroom mirror.

> *This is a trustworthy saying, and everyone should accept it: "Christ Jesus came into the world to save sinners"—and I am the worst of them all. But God had mercy on me so that Christ Jesus could use me as a prime example of his great patience with even the worst sinners. Then others will realize that they, too, can believe in him and receive eternal life* (NLT).

Justine wants the immortal, invisible, eternal God to be honored and to receive glory for ever and ever! Justine formerly worshiped her rules. Not any more. Now Justine wants to worship God.

Delight/Joy

When rightness-oriented friends like Justine repent they come to love true holiness. Justine once believed her rightness reflected holiness. Now she realizes her rightness didn't reflect holiness at all; it reflected pride. Her orientation was all about following her rules, and Justine thought following her rules would bring her happiness. She didn't care about relationships as much as she cared about keeping rules.

Genuine holiness is appealing to others because it is the essence of God. To be holy is to have perfect freedom from all evil. This is both lovely and desirable! To be perfectly free from all evil—from rape, murder, war, selfishness, and greediness; from unkindness, slander, dishonesty, and hatred; from impatience, harshness, wickedness, and from pride. We've all been hurt by others practicing these sins against us or against those we love. No wonder holiness brings joy; even the thought of being free of these evils is delightful.

Seen in Action

As a rightness-oriented friend, Justine treated everyone around her in a proud, condescending way. When she repented she began to humbly acknowledge her weaknesses and her need for God's grace. One area in which Justine demonstrated humility was in her small-group Bible study. She admitted to the others that she had been functioning in a very arrogant and self-righteous way. She confessed that rather than coming to Bible study to learn, she had really just been coming out of religious duty. Accordingly, she had an "I already know all this" attitude and was critical of everything and everyone.

Justine asked for her Bible study group to pray that she would be aware of each time she thought or acted in a self-righteous way. She also requested that the members of the group confront her if they saw her going back to her old habits. Justine suggested several clues which might alert them that she was functioning according to old habits. These clues included:

- Critical statements about others
- Impatience
- Unthankfulness
- Speaking about others as if they were idiots or incompetent
- Acting as if her life was busier, more hectic, or harder than everyone else's life
- General, non-specific prayer requests for herself
- Prayer requests that focused solely on others' weaknesses
- Prayer requests that focused on physical needs

Justine has repented of her rightness attitude toward her neighbor Ryan, who frequently doesn't park in his designated spot at their apartment complex. Justine was overcome with remorse when she realized that when she got angry because Ryan wasn't following the rules, she never gave any thought to where he might spend eternity. She was more grieved over Ryan's wrong choice of a parking spot than she was concerned about whether he would spend eternity in hell. For all she knew, Ryan would face the wrath of God for his sins and she was concerned about a petty parking spot. By her lack of compassion, she was nonverbally communicating, "Go to hell; just don't park in the wrong parking space."

As a genuine friend, Justine has begun to look for ways to serve rather than ways to condemn. Now, as she backs out of her parking space and sees Ryan's car in the wrong spot, she prays for Ryan, asking God to bless him. She prays that God will give her opportunities to show His love to this precious soul.

The genuine and authentic friend sees her sins as large in comparison to the sins of others. In the past, Justine would minimize her faults while maximizing the faults of others. She was impatient and critical. She was proud. She was judgmental. She held grudges. And she didn't think any of these sinful attitudes were a big deal. In her mind, she always had a good reason for being impatient, critical, proud, or judgmental.

Now Justine has taken Matthew 7:3-5 to heart:

> *Why do you look at the speck of sawdust in your brother's eye and pay no attention to the plank in your own eye? How can you say to your brother, "Let me take the speck out of your eye," when all the time there is a plank in your own eye? You hypocrite, first take the plank out of your own eye, and then you will see clearly to remove the speck from your brother's eye.*

Seeing her sins as a plank has helped Justine treat others with much more sensitivity. As one wise man has said, "Once you've had your own eye operation, you become a bit gentler when it's time to take the speck out of someone else's eye."

One of the changes Justine's friends have noticed is that she has put on meekness. In the past, Justine insisted that things be done her way (the right way). Her sister had to put her dishes in the dishwasher as soon as she was finished with them, her clients had to accept her color palette, and Justine's apartment had to be cleaned the way she thought best.

Now Justine wants to be like her big brother, Christ. He gave up His rights in order to minister. Christ could have insisted on His rights, yet He displayed meekness throughout His life:

- He could have insisted on having a royal physician present at His birth.

- He could have insisted on having the shepherds take a bath before coming to visit.

- He could have insisted His parents obey Him while He was growing up.

- He could have insisted that the people in His hometown build Him a palace and bow down whenever He appeared on the streets.

- He could have insisted on having Secret Service to protect Him from death threats.

- He could have insisted on a lineage without prostitutes and murderers.

- He could have insisted we pay the penalty for our sins.

When Justine's church began a Bible study for addicts, Justine was the first to sign up. On the first night, as every person introduced themselves and gave their reason for joining the study, Justine said this, "In the past I never saw a reason to join a Bible study like this. I was glad there were Bible studies for addicts—I wanted them to get their lives cleaned up and begin doing right. In fact, many of you may have heard me make condescending comments about how glad I was the people in those studies were doing so well.

"Another reason I would never have been part of a study like this was because, in my pride, I would never have wanted anyone to think I was sinful and certainly not sinful enough to have an addiction. However, I've come to realize that I've been addicted to my pride. Not only that but my addiction is much worse than any addiction to alcohol or drugs. God says He detests pride (Proverbs 6:17) and in the list of things He detests, God doesn't mention addictions. So, I need to be part of this group—as a participant—not as a mentor or leader, as I formerly believed."

What Others Experience

When rightness-oriented friends become genuine friends they openly admit their struggles and seek forgiveness from others. This is sometimes astounding to those who have known them as a rightness-oriented friend. In the past, the rightness-oriented friend never seemed to have anything for which she needed to repent; she always portrayed herself as right. Nevertheless, while her actions may not have been overtly sinful, like the Pharisees, her heart was despicable. Right actions were done with wrong motives. The rightness-oriented friend was very adept at positioning herself to look blameless, all the while selfishly pursuing her own desires.

Part of the repentance process usually includes seeking forgiveness, not only from God, but from others. Justine's friend, Elaine, was flabbergasted when Justine called to ask forgiveness.

"Elaine," Justine said, "when you came to our design firm, you clearly communicated your preferences regarding the color in your bedroom. I responded arrogantly to your request, deciding my opinions were better than yours. I insisted on doing things my way. I was wrong to treat you like that. I should always be seeking to put the interests of others first, but it's especially wrong when you have hired me to work for you to insist that things should be done my way.

"Not only that but I schemed how to present my ideas to you so that you would acquiesce to my desires. I communicated that the colors you chose were out of date and over used. I tried to pressure you to accept my color palette by appealing to a desire not to seem old-fashioned and out of touch.

"It was wrong not to put your interests first. It was wrong to try to manipulate you. I had a proud and condescending attitude. I am very sorry.

"I've gone back and developed a design plan using the color scheme you desired. I'd like to waive all charges for any time I've spent on your job."

Justine concluded by asking, "Will you forgive me?"

Prior to this, Elaine had harbored a certain amount of distaste for Justine. Now wheels were set in motion for a genuine friendship to develop. Working on the master bedroom became a pleasure for Elaine and Justine. Justine would suggest different approaches but not in a superior way. With Justine's direction, Elaine began to understand how to think about and organize design projects. As they continued working together, it became clear that Elaine really possessed a natural aptitude for design work. Elaine's tastes and preferences ran more along classic and timeless lines, while Justine's tastes and preferences were more modern; nevertheless Elaine's taste was exquisite.

When they finished the project, Justine suggested that Elaine work with her firm as a consultant. Elaine's tastes could add a wonderful complement to Justine's style. Justine believed that by collaborating they could better serve the clients who used the services of the design firm.

Another area in which others are experiencing beautiful changes in their friendship with Justine is in her readiness to extend mercy and grace. As a rightness-oriented friend, Justine thought the answer to every problem was to come up with a rule to follow. Rules were Justine's form of a pill for every ill. Too much time spent on personal business at work? Make a rule that computers can only be used for company business. Employees not staying within their budget? Make a rule that all expenses must be approved before a purchase can be made. Employees taking the closest parking space to the door rather than leaving the best spots for clients? Make a rule that employees must park in designated spaces at the back of the parking lot.

Now Justine realizes that actions come from the heart, and simply making up rules won't change the heart. Now, instead of sending out an office memo to everyone in the company with the latest rule, Justine is more likely to patiently address issues individually. This is harder than creating rules, but Justine has learned to care more about what is going on in the heart of her employees than simply producing employees who look good on the outside but really care little about the people whom they have the opportunity to serve.

In the past, Justine demanded perfection from her employees and used intimidation and manipulation to achieve her goals. Justine still holds high standards for excellence, but she has taken to heart Christ's rebuke of the Pharisees in Matthew 23:23-24. In that passage, Christ pointed out that the Pharisees focused on getting incidental issues just right, but ignored more important things like justice, mercy, and faithfulness.

In the past, Justine frequently expected her employees to work overtime in order to get the details of a presentation just perfect. It wasn't important to Justine that she was asking her employees to regularly neglect their families or other obligations outside of work in order to achieve a spectacular presentation. Justine didn't care if her employees were disheartened when she focused on nitpicky imperfections while ignoring the hours of sacrificial service they devoted to their work.

Now, Justine shows concern for employees. Justine has lengthened the time estimates she gives to her clients rather than continually demanding her employees put in overtime. Justine makes it clear she wants her employees to serve their families well, just as she wants her employees to serve the company well during work hours.

Over time, Justine's design firm has flourished. The productivity of her employees has increased, in part because they no longer have to battle the demoralizing influence of a harsh boss. Even beyond that, however, God has blessed Justine's desire for genuine holiness and entrusted her with more opportunities and increased revenue. She has generously shared all this with those who work for her. Working for Justine has come to be very desirable.

Chapter 16
From Pleasure-Oriented to Genuine and Authentic Friendships

For a friend who has been enslaved to pleasure-oriented friendships, doing a relationship U-turn brings the glorious freedom of meaningful relationships. When Solomon tried living life for his pleasure, he eventually experienced the disillusionment that led him to proclaim, *"Everything is meaningless"* (Ecclesiastes 2:11). If the wisest man in the Old Testament wasn't smart enough to figure out how to make pleasure-oriented living worthwhile, I think it's safe to say no one else will be able to either.

Being liberated from a meaningless existence allows the genuine and authentic friend to pursue relationships that are rich and substantial. Relationships in the past were inane, based solely on the pleasure of the moment. Thus, a lot of talk occurred, but without much substance. Pleasure-oriented friends are able to talk for hours about entertainment and sports or other things of little personal consequence. They can often trade sarcastic put downs and clever witticisms, but they don't develop relationships where self-disclosure takes place. They can analyze the latest news and dissect the performance of their favorite sports team, but they never get beyond that to the difficulties and struggles going on in their hearts. Such topics are not considered pleasurable.

As a genuine friend, discussions about the news, sports, and weather still occur, but conversations are not confined to these topics. The genuine friend desires to go beyond casual relationships. She wants to enter the suffering and distress her friends may experience in order to minister to them. As she does this, her relationships take on a richness she has never before experienced.

Heart's Desire

The richest relationship desired by the former pleasure-oriented friend is a friendship with God. Unquestionably substantial, there will always be more to experience in a relationship with Him. As Randy Alcorn says in his book, *Heaven*, "God is mesmerizing to the depths of His being and those depths will never be exhausted."[66]

The well of friendship with God will never be totally plumbed. Paul learned this in his friendship with God. It led Paul to exclaim: Oh, the depth of the riches of the wisdom and knowledge of God! How unsearchable his judgments, and his paths beyond tracing out! (Romans 11:33). Just when you think you understand God, you realize there's more.

In Tom Clancy's *Hunt for Red October*, the US navy engages in a desperate search for a Russian nuclear submarine, captained by the USSR's best captain, Marko Ramius. Driven by the fear that Ramius plans to launch a nuclear attack from the *Red October*, the US Navy dedicates its best resources to tracking the Russian submarine.

The stealthiness of the *Red October* and skill of Ramius seem to promise certain elusion until CIA analyst, Jack Ryan is brought in. Ryan has studied Ramius so thoroughly that the US Joint Chiefs of Staff are willing to gamble that he can predict Ramius' intent. One of the reasons Clancy's plot is such a page turner is the suspense of whether Ryan will be able to accurately "trace out" the Soviet's intent. While Ryan is successful in his quest to figure out the intent of Captain Ramius, he would have failed miserably had God been the captain of the Russian submarine. God's paths are beyond tracing out.

Who could have predicted that God would send His Son to die for His enemies? We have trouble sacrificing for our best friend. Who could have

---

[66] Alcorn, Randy, *Heaven* (Carol Stream, IL: Tyndale, 2006), p. 198.

predicted that Christ would stick to His guns when He was tempted after 40 days in the wilderness without food? We complain after we miss one meal. Who could have predicted that Christ wouldn't pull the plug on His plan when He was mocked, spit upon and beaten? We react sinfully when a driver cuts us off. What would seem to be much more predictable is that God would annihilate His enemies. What would seem to be much more predictable is that God would toss us out on our ear. What would seem to be much more predictable is that God would start over with a creation that wouldn't rebel against Him. Isn't that what we would do if we were God? But God's ways are beyond tracing out. No wonder Paul ends Romans 11 by exclaiming, *"To Him be the glory forever!"*

In her friendships with others, the authentic friend wants her friends to know the eternal pleasures provided by God, not the momentary pleasure of sin. She has great compassion for those who don't know Christ as Savior, because they will experience God's displeasure forever in hell.

As Ellie, the pleasure-oriented friend we met in chapter 8, grew in genuine friendship, she became more sensitive to the awfulness of hell. Ellie learned that when sinners are sentenced to depart from God, they are sentenced to depart from everything and anything that is good. Because every good and perfect gift is from God (James 1:17), those who die without knowing Christ will be deprived of all good. They will never, ever enjoy a good day or good thing again. [67]

Understanding these truths has caused Ellie to be very sober. It breaks Ellie's heart to think that any of her friends might experience hell. She longs for her friends to trust in Christ and be saved.

Acceptable Cost

My brother-in-law (as well as all my other family members) came to my college graduation. How fun is that for a guy? Going to the graduation of your sister-in-law? Not! Nevertheless, Tom treated me like a genuine friend by attending the graduation ceremony.

The genuineness of Tom's friendship is magnified when you learn that Tom was offered free tickets to the Indy 500 that day. I'm not a big racing fan, but even I can understand that going to your sister-in-law's graduation instead of going to the Indy 500 is a significant sacrifice. Genuine friends

---

[67] Venning, Ralph, *The Sinfulness of Sin* (Carlisle, PA: The Banner of Truth Trust, 1993)

are willing to give up what might be pleasurable to them in order to bring pleasure to others.

The genuine friend has learned that there are two kinds of pleasure; the momentary pleasure of sin mentioned in Job 20:5 or the eternal pleasures of God declared in Psalm 16:11. The genuine friend is happy to sacrifice momentary pleasure for eternal pleasure.

Genuine friends are so disgusted with living empty lives that the thought of returning to a pleasure-oriented lifestyle is repugnant. This will not make sense to many of their old friends. The genuine friend may find that she is living out 1 Peter 4:4 with friends who think it strange that she doesn't plunge with them into the same flood of dissipation, and heap abuse on her. In the midst of such abuse, the genuine friend is encouraged by 1 Peter 3:17. *"It is better, if it is God's will, to suffer for doing good than for doing evil."* The genuine friend is willing to be misunderstood or ridiculed by those with whom she formerly partied.

Joy/Delight

The greatest delight of former pleasure-oriented friends, after they repent of their pleasure orientation, is to know God more and more intimately. They long to know the things that give God pleasure.

For her current Bible study, Ellie has made it her goal to find one new character quality every week that brings God pleasure. Using her concordance she has looked up verses on delight and pleasure. For each reference, she studies the verses around it and the cross references. Ellie works on each quality for at least a week. So far, Ellie has put the following qualities on her list of things that give God pleasure: faithfulness, self-discipline, honesty, humility, a contrite heart, showing mercy, obedience, living a life of love, generosity, forgiveness and holiness.

When Ellie adds something to her list, she makes a plan for how she can demonstrate that quality in her life in concrete, measurable ways. For example, when Ellie learned that God loves faithfulness, she realized she had to change the way she thought about making commitments.
First, she realized she had to start keeping the commitments she made. In the past, Ellie had made and kept commitments only when she felt like it. To help her please God, Ellie memorized Psalm 15:1, 4: *"LORD, who may dwell in your sanctuary? Who may live on your holy hill? ... (He) who*

keeps his oath even when it hurts." Then Ellie went to ask forgiveness from a number of people for not keeping her commitments.

Soon Ellie decided to develop a schedule to reflect God-given priorities so she could fulfill the responsibilities given to her by God. Her schedule included her job, church, study time to know God better, household chores, her family, sleep, rest, etc. Once she had plugged all these responsibilities into her weekly schedule, she made a plan for the time that remained.

She calculated the amount of free time she had each week that was previously given to satisfying her pleasure orientation. She determined that she wanted to commit 30% of this time to a regularly scheduled ministry to others. Since she had training as a lifeguard, Ellie decided to volunteer at the local community center pool every week.

Another 30% of her free time would be for serving opportunities that were hard to preplan. For example, she could use that time to fix a meal for someone, visit someone in the hospital, help one of her friends move, or call someone who needed encouragement.

The remaining 40% of her unscheduled time, Ellie kept open for unforeseen appointments and incidents. If that time wasn't used up, she planned to use the time for leisure.

Creating a plan for her time has helped Ellie in making commitments and in sticking to the commitments she makes. Her schedule is essentially "My plan for using the time God has given me to please Him."

Seen in Action

"Hey Ellie, do you want to go to the new downtown restaurant and then to the midnight screening of that movie you wanted to see?" asked Jacob.

"I can't tonight. I've already committed to lifeguard at the community center from 7 - 9:30. If I go to a movie after that I won't want to get up for church."

"Since when did you get so religious? Church will still be there next week, you can go then," was Jacob's pushback. "I don't know why you lifeguard at that community center anyway. You should tell them that if they're not going to pay you, you can't do it. What's up with you these days, you're no fun anymore."

Jacob's comment stung, but Ellie stood her ground in keeping her commitment. Although she knew she was likely to be the target of some gossip and sarcasm, Ellie found it completely satisfying to be someone others could depend on, even if it meant missing the movie.

On Sunday, Ellie arrived about ten minutes early for her Adult Bible Fellowship.

"Hey, girlfriend, how was lifeguarding last night?" asked Macy.

"Lifeguarding was a blast. Watching those little kids paddle around in their swimees is so much fun. It's neat to see them get more and more comfortable in the water. I remember how scared I was when I first started swimming. I hated putting my head underwater. The community center pool has lots of great features that help kids really enjoy learning to swim."

"I take it you didn't have to rescue anyone."

"No, everything was calm—nice and uneventful. Listen to that, would you ever have expected to hear me use "nice" and "uneventful" in the same sentence. In the old days, uneventful meant no fun. Remove yourself from that situation ASAP."

"It's good not being controlled by that anymore, huh?" said Macy, as class started.

Ellie took notes on what was taught in class and the main worship service. Later she called her class teacher to ask a follow-up question, enthused about how cool it was to understand God better.

Tuesday night Ellie went to her friend Monica's house. Monica's mom had been diagnosed with cancer six months ago. Treatment proved to be ineffective, and Monica had asked her mother to move into her home so that she could care for her. Ellie went over every week to give Monica a chance to get out. In the process, Ellie formed a deep friendship with Monica's mom, Mrs. Grayson. After Monica left, Ellie and Mrs. Grayson picked up Randy Alcorn's book on heaven, which they had been reading together. This had stimulated many talks about eternity.

"In the past, I would have fled from a relationship with you," commented Ellie. "Knowing that you were dying, the only thing I would have known to do is encourage you to try to find some new medical treatment in the hope that you would be cured. While I'm certainly not against a medical treatment that would cure you, I've come to understand that hope is not based on finding a cure, hope is based on our Savior and Lord. We can talk about your death with tears and joy at the same time."

"I agree," said Mrs. Grayson. "Christ said He was going to prepare a place for me. My dying means I'll be in heaven. Do you remember the analogy we read in the *Heaven* book? Alcorn said this:

> When Nanci was pregnant with each of our girls, she and I prepared a place for them. We decorated the room, picked out the right wallpaper, set up the crib just so, and selected the perfect blankets. The quality of the place we prepared for our daughters was limited only by our skills, resources, and imagination.
>
> In Heaven, what kind of a place can we expect our Lord to have prepared for us? Because He isn't limited and He loves us even more than we love our children, I think we can expect to find the best place ever made by anyone, for anyone, in the history of the universe. The God who commends hospitality will not be outdone in His hospitality to us.[68]

Mrs. Grayson continued, "I'm eager to taste God's hospitality! In fact, I've never looked forward to any resort vacation as much as I'm looking forward to heaven."

"For someone like me, who's been consumed with pleasure, the idea of being with God and experiencing the eternal pleasures He promises in Psalm 16:11 tempts me to be envious of you," said Ellie.
She continued, "I think at one time I believed heaven would be boring. Therefore I functioned as if I'd better squeeze in all the pleasure I could get in this life, because in heaven I'd just sit on a cloud and play a harp. Now I realize I believed a lie. Satan would love to have me believe heaven

---

[68] Alcorn, *Heaven*, p. 163.

is boring and undesirable."

Mrs. Grayson nodded. "Satan has done such a good job spreading his lies that we reject the idea that fun originated with God. We think heaven will be boring because we think sin is fun and righteousness is boring. In fact, freedom from sin will mean freedom to be what God intended, freedom to find greater joy and fun in everything.[69]

"The best is yet to come. We haven't yet watched our most exciting sports event, we haven't yet tasted the best meal we'll ever have, we haven't yet played the most fun game we'll ever play, and we haven't laughed the hardest we'll ever laugh. God invented pleasure and it will never be 'same old, same old' with Him."

When Monica returned, Ellie said to her, "Your mom is a very godly woman. She's been such an encouragement to me. Even though the chemo has caused her to lose her hair and she's bloated from the water retention, I think she's one of the most beautiful women I've ever met."

As Ellie left Monica's and drove home, her route took her past her favorite mall. In the past, Ellie would have automatically slowed down and turned into the mall. Tonight however, she kept driving. When Ellie began living to please God, she realized her pursuit of pleasure had caused her to run up thousands of dollars in credit card bills. Although she was able to make the monthly payments, Ellie became dissatisfied with all the money she was paying in interest. Now, she desires to use the resources entrusted to her by God to give generously. Previously, her attitude had always been, "When I make more money, I'll start giving." However, even though Ellie had received annual salary increases, she simply increased her standard of living. She didn't see the increases as an opportunity to be generous.

When Ellie learned Psalm 24:1—"*The earth is the Lord's, and everything in it*"—she began to think about her income and possessions in a new way. She realized, God owns everything, I own nothing. As a result, Ellie went to work to eliminate her debt. She reviewed her spending and made it her goal to get out of debt in 12 months. In order to do this, Ellie got rid of her premium cable TV package, switched to a cheaper cell phone plan, canceled her lawn care service, stopped eating out for entertainment, and

---

[69] Alcorn, Randy, *Heaven* (Carol Stream, IL: Tyndal, 2004).

advertised for a roommate. Once she gets out of debt, Ellie plans to use the money formerly tied up in paying off debt to increase her giving.

To help herself stick to her plan, Ellie has quit going shopping with her friends because she realized that she usually made unwise financial decisions when she spent time at the mall. Now, she is more likely to invite her friends over to fix a meal for someone who's sick or just had a new baby. For the first time ever, Ellie is learning how much fun it is to serve with other people.

What Others Experience

As Ellie has grown spiritually, she has been surprised to realize how often she participated in gossip. As a pleasure-oriented friend, gossip had been a routine part of her conversation. She and her friends habitually dished up whatever tantalizing morsels they knew about their friends or enemies. At the time, Ellie enjoyed sharing information that made someone else look bad.

Ellie's friend, Kylie, was initially annoyed when Ellie quit gossiping with her. In the past few weeks however, she has come to appreciate Ellie's refusal to gossip. After Kylie got arrested for drunk driving, she was hurt by the way her friends enjoyed the details of her arrest and fed on the fact that she did jail time.

"Now I appreciate knowing that you don't participate in gossip anymore," Kylie told Ellie. "The first time you called 'time out' when I started to gossip about my mother-in-law, I was mad. I didn't see anything wrong with telling you bad things about her if they were true. In my mind, what I said about her would only have been wrong if I were lying. When you told me, 'You know, that would really hurt your mother-in-law if she knew what we were saying,' I just blew it off and decided you had gotten way too religious. In fact, I convinced myself that you were just some weirdo fanatic, and I wasn't doing anything wrong.

"Now that my arrest has been printed in the paper, I've become very sensitive to what others are saying about me. Because we always talk about others, I'm pretty certain all my friends are savoring this new piece of gossip. Some of them are even bold enough to ask me for details, like what my blood alcohol content was.

"Ellie, I'm ashamed of what happened, but everyone else just seems to see it as another morsel to savor and make them feel better about themselves. I no longer see you as some religious fanatic. I'm grateful to know you're protecting my reputation and not telling everyone how belligerent I was when the cops pulled me over."

Kylie continued, "I know you told me before, but what are the two rules you follow in deciding whether you should call a 'time out'?"

Ellie responded, "My two rules are:

> 1. would this person be hurt if she heard what I was saying about her? If so, I need to call a 'time-out.'
>
> 2. am I part of the problem or part of the solution? If I'm not part of the solution, I need to call 'time out.'"

"I'm going to start using those rules," declared Kylie.

As Ellie has learned to control her tongue, she has become less sarcastic in her speech. Formerly, she could have been called the Queen of Zingers. She could quickly shoot off one liners which, while terribly funny, always had a bite to them. If anyone got hurt, it was easy to say, "I was just kidding."

As Ellie studied the qualities of the Proverbs 31 virtuous woman, she discovered verse 26—*"on her tongue is the law of kindness"* (NKJV). She realized that the law of kindness wasn't on her tongue. The law on Ellie's tongue was getting others to laugh, often at the expense of someone else. Right then, she decided that it was more important to be kind than to be funny. God doesn't command that we be funny; He does command kindness. As a result, her friends feel much less vulnerable with her. They no longer fear that their weaknesses will be the subject of a wisecrack. Instead, Ellie regularly praises the strengths of her friends.

As Ellie has grown in authentic friendship, she has become a friend who enters into the suffering and trials her friends' experience. Now she is there for them when they go through hard times. She has been there for her friends when they've been in the hospital, when a family member has died, when they broke up with their boyfriend, when their basement flooded, when the cat brought in a live mouse, and when they got laid off.

When someone is suffering, Ellie does more than just show up and quietly mourn with them (which is significant in and of itself). Ellie is able to offer genuine hope and encouragement. She has been encouraged by what she has learned from books like *Trusting God* by Jerry Bridges, *Tearful Celebration* by James Means, and *It's Not Fair* by Wayne Mack and Deborah Howard.[70] It's not unusual when one of Ellie's friends goes through a trial for that friend to receive a set of index cards from Ellie with encouraging verses Ellie has printed on them. When Ellie calls to learn how her friends are doing, she often takes the time to pray with them on the phone, asking God to strengthen them and help them bear their load in a way that glorifies her precious Savior. Ellie's friends have come to turn to her as a trusted friend in both pain and pleasure. She has become a friend who loves God with all her heart, soul, mind and strength, and who loves others as herself.

---

[70] Bridges, Jerry, *Trusting God*. (Colorado Springs, CO: Navpress, 1988).
Means, James, *A Tearful Celebration* (Portland, OR: Multnomah, 1985).
Mack, Wayne & Howard, Deborah, *It's Not Fair* (Phillipsburg, NJ: Presbyterian and Reformed Publishing Co, 2008).

Chapter 17
From Comfort-Oriented to Genuine
and Authentic Friendships

Whopper Sacrifice vs. Michelle Hartman

Did you hear about the Whopper Sacrifice on Facebook? Apparently Burger King ran an application on Facebook early in 2009 that rewarded people with a coupon for a Whopper if they removed 10 friends from their friend list. Each time a friend was excommunicated, the application sent a notice to the banished party explaining that the user's love for the "friend" was less than his or her zeal for the Whopper. The Whopper Sacrifice only lasted for a week, but during that time 82,000 users had sacrificed more than 230,000 friends.

Then there's Michelle Hartman. Michelle is my niece and she was motivated not to sacrifice friends from Facebook, but to sacrifice her kidney for the husband of one her dearest friends. I asked Michelle some questions about her decision to sacrifice her kidney. Here are the answers Michelle gave me.

How did you and Kimberly become friends?

Kimberly and I were introduced when we were 3 years old. We went to preschool together and stayed friends ever since. While we only went to the same school until third grade, we went to the same church and were in youth group together growing up. We have been there for each other for all the different stages in our lives. Our friendship has remained strong even after Kimberly married her husband Chris, and had a baby daughter, Ava.

Why did you decide to donate your kidney to Kimberly's husband?

Shortly after a trip to Chicago to visit Kimberly, Chris, and Ava, Kimberly called and let me know that Chris was in the hospital with kidney issues (a complication of his Crohn's Disease). At that point they didn't know if he would need a transplant, but without hesitation I told her that I'd get tested if he did. There wasn't ever really a thought not to. We found out a few weeks later that he would need a transplant, and I started the testing process from Denver. We found out that I was an initial match.

What were the risks of the surgery?

Obviously, worst-case scenario would have been death. This was a long surgery to remove an organ, so the doctors never let me forget (death) could happen. More likely risks were infection, internal bleeding, or "nicking" the intestine with the knife as they were going towards the kidney. Also, I knew that I would have to take good care of the other kidney afterwards.

The risks didn't deter Michelle and she scheduled the 8-hour surgery to remove her kidney, so that it could be transplanted into Chris.

How long was the recovery?

(After the surgery) I was in the hospital 2 or 3 days. I stayed at Kimberly and Chris' house for a little over a month. After about a month, Kimberly drove me back to Denver, where I continued to recover for another few weeks. At about 8 weeks, I went back to work part-time, and felt back to normal at about 3 months.

How is Kimberly's husband doing today?

> While my kidney worked initially, there was a surgical bleed which caused it to start to fail. Within 2 days, the kidney had completely died and was removed from Chris.

> Three months later, Chris was given a kidney by his uncle. This time it went flawlessly, and he is doing great! Last year, he ran a half-marathon. (He had never been a runner, and hadn't even run 3 miles before the transplant.) He has now taken up adventure racing and recently did a 12 mile trek through deep snow with his dog. He is doing his best to eat well and exercise to take good care of this one. The average donated kidney lasts about 10-12 years. Since he is 38, he is likely to need a couple more before the end of his life, but wants to make each one last as long as possible.

> Kimberly has always been like a sister to me, and so I consider her family like my own. It was never even a thought that I wouldn't help little Ava to have her daddy as long as possible if I could do anything about it. More than ever, we both consider each other, as well as Chris and Ava, true family.

Unquestionably, Michelle is not a comfort-oriented friend. Michelle is a genuine and authentic friend.

Heart's Desire

Rather than living for ease and comfort, the comfort-oriented friend who becomes a genuine friend, desires to sacrifice for others and to love others deeply. Paul had this kind of love for the Jews. In Romans chapter 9, Paul tells his beloved friends, *"I have great sorrow and unceasing anguish in my heart. For I could wish that I myself were cursed and cut off from Christ for the sake of my brothers, those of my own race."*

Paul loved so deeply he indicated a willingness to go to hell if it would enable his friends to spend eternity in heaven. Can you think of friends who would be willing to make that sacrifice for you? Can you think of friends you'd be willing to suffer for in hell in order that they could go to heaven? Paul's friendship was genuine and authentic.

The desire to love others deeply and sacrifice for them springs from a deep desire to be like Christ. Christ laid down his life in order that we could become His friends. Being a friend like Christ results in a growing desire to love and sacrifice for others.

Acceptable Cost

In chapter 9 we met Rose, a comfort-oriented friend. For Rose, and those like her, the price to become a genuine and authentic friend is giving up living in their comfort zone. Comfort-oriented friends are accustomed to doing only what is easy for them. They live for themselves, doing only what they like to do until pressure causes them to change. (Note: This doesn't mean they don't ever do anything that might be considered hard. They may do hard things if they have been so trained to perform those things that they no longer seem hard. For example, comfort-oriented friends may have been trained as a child to keep their room clean. They may continue this practice as an adult because continuous training has made keeping their room clean a relatively easy task. Keeping the room clean may seem easier than the discomfort of living with disorder.)

When comfort-oriented friends become genuine and authentic friends they are willing to pay the price of being uncomfortable. They are willing to give up doing things the easy way. They are willing to do hard things.

Like other comfort-oriented friends who repent and become genuine and authentic friends, Rose is now willing to sacrifice for her friends. Rose has come to cherish John 15:13: *"Greater love has no man than this, than that a man lay down his life for his friends."*

Rose knows that ordinarily she won't be asked to die physically for her friends. She has learned, however, that it can seem as hard as dying to lay down her desires for ease and comfort in order to be a genuine friend. She has learned that getting out of bed to help someone move is a form of laying down her plans for her friends. She has learned that reaching out to new people, when she'd rather simply join the cluster of friends she already knows well, is a form of dying to her fear of leaving her comfort zone. And she has learned that controlling her tongue and building up others, rather than complaining, is a form of dying to her flesh.

Whereas in the past, Rose feared having to exert effort on behalf of her friends, she is now more than willing to wear herself out for the benefit of her friends. Not only that, she is also willing to sacrifice for her enemies. Because her best friend Christ loved her when she was His enemy, she prays for love for those she would consider her enemies.

Joy/Delight

Rose's greatest joy, upon becoming an authentic friend, has been to become like Christ by being a servant. Rose longs to hear these words from God someday, "Well done, good and faithful servant."

As a friend who wants to be genuine and authentic, Rose is willing to expend her energy, time, skills, and resources for others. She embraces this sacrifice because she wants to be like Christ. Like Christ, she is now willing to become poor so that others can become rich. Rose has a beautifully framed copy of 2 Corinthians 8:9 hanging in her family room.

> *For you know the grace of our Lord Jesus Christ, that though he was rich, yet for your sakes he became poor, so that you through his poverty might become rich.*

Becoming poor so that others can become rich is not only an acceptable cost, the thought of richly blessing others causes genuine friends great delight.

Seen in Action

As she has grown in becoming an authentic friend, Rose has benefitted from being mentored by a wonderful, godly woman. Her mentor, Mrs. Cryan, is loved and respected by many and has mentored a number of young "Roses" over the years. Mrs. Cryan suggested she and Rose search the Scriptures to learn what it means to be a servant. They started in John chapter 13.

"Rose, suppose you were responsible for exposing a drug ring in our city and, as a result, gang members are now determined to kill you. In fact, they have posted notice on the internet that they plan to execute you before the end of the week. If you were having dinner with a group of your friends at one of their homes when all this came to a climax, what would you do?" asked Mrs. Cryan.

"I'd probably beg my friends to hide me somewhere," Rose answered.

"Would you care if your friends were wearing muddy shoes when they came to dinner? Would you clean their shoes so they wouldn't track mud all over your friend's carpet?" continued Mrs. Cryan.

"No, the only thing I'd care about at that point was what was going to happen to me," replied Rose.

"I think we'd all be like that," said Mrs. Cryan. "That's why John 13 is so shocking. On the night He was betrayed, Christ wasn't focused on Himself. He served his friends."

"That's so totally not like me," reported Rose. "I know I would have expected my friends to make it all about me."

"That's the thing about being a Christ follower. Christ didn't die to tweak what was already a pretty good package. Christ died to make us radically different. So radically different that we'd not only serve our friends, we'd serve our enemies even in extreme circumstances. Remember, Judas was at that dinner with Christ, too."

"I've got a lot of growing to do," said Rose. "That really stretches me."

"It stretches me too. I think we're usually content with minor cosmetic changes when God wants radical transformation. If we hold the door open for people coming behind us and serve in the church nursery, we think we get it. We think we're servants. And we think that by doing those acts of service we do not have to be servants at other times. It's somebody else's turn. We have the nature of a master who sometimes does a little bit of serving. But in Philippians 2:5-7 we're told our attitude is to be like Christ's who took the very *nature* of a servant.

"To have the *nature* of a servant means you are a servant in the very core of your being. It's the essence of who you are. It means you are continuously working to bring profit to the person you're serving. You see it as your duty to make another person prosperous. You labor to make another person rich. You apply yourself for the benefit of someone else. You function for someone else's welfare. You exert yourself for another's good. You toil for another person's betterment. And you do it all the time because that's your nature; that's who you are," elaborated Mrs. Cryan.

Rose struggled. "Does that mean I should become a doormat?" Rose probed.

"Let me answer that by asking a couple of questions," responded Mrs. Cryan

"Does taking the very nature of a servant mean you do all the serving so everyone else can do all the relaxing?" asked Mrs. Cryan. She paused while Rose thought about her question and then continued, "To whom is Philippians 2:5-7 addressed?"

"Every believer," responded Rose. "So, what you're saying is that in order to be like Christ *every* believer needs to take the nature of a servant."

"Yes, God wants every individual whom He has called to be like Christ. To have the same attitude, to have the same desires, and to have the same goal," said Mrs. Cryan. "And Christ was a servant."

"If you had a sister in Christ who wanted you to do all the serving while she did all the relaxing, how could you best serve her?" asked Mrs. Cryan.

"By helping her to become a servant as well," Rose concluded.

"So, would you be a doormat if you did that?" asked Mrs. Cryan.

"No, I don't think so," replied Rose.

"Now, let me ask you this? If Christ did want you to be a doormat, would you do it?" queried Mrs. Cryan.

"Yes," Rose now said unresistingly.

"Why?"

"Because being like Christ is the treasure I'd sell everything to get. If that's what Christ wanted, I'd realize I've never properly understood the beauty and value of a doormat," responded Rose.

"That was a really, really mature answer," said Mrs. Cryan. "It's clear you want to be like Christ."

As they continued their study, Mrs. Cryan and Rose developed a self-evaluation questionnaire to use as an accountability tool. They titled the questionnaire, "Do I Have a Servant's Heart?"

Do I Have a Servant's Heart?

Each of the following continuums is to help you examine your heart. The anchoring statements next to 1 represent the low end of the continuum (a comfort-oriented heart). The anchoring statements next to 4 represent the high end of the continuum (a servant's heart). Pick the number on the scale of 1-4 that best reflects your heart.

1. I serve simply because it is expected.   1 2 3 4   I serve to show love and gratitude for God.

2. I serve simply because others are doing it.   1 2 3 4   I serve for Jesus' sake.

3. I have to be persuaded or pled with in order to serve.   1 2 3 4   I voluntarily take the servant's role.

4. I have to be told what to do.   1 2 3 4   I take initiative in serving.

5. I expect to serve according to my schedule.   1 2 3 4   I adapt my schedule to meet others needs.

6. I serve only when I feel like serving.   1 2 3 4   I serve whether I feel like it or not.

7. I begrudge the time I spend serving and wish I could be doing something else instead.   1 2 3 4   I have a joyful attitude about serving.

8. I make statements like, "I wish I didn't have to do this tonight."   1 2 3 4   I thank God for the opportunity to be like Christ.

9. God gets only leftover time.	1 2 3 4	Service is a priority.
10. God gets only leftover effort.	1 2 3 4	Service cost me something.
11. My friends would say that I seek my own good.	1 2 3 4	My friends would say that they have prospered because of me.
12. Self-denial is rare in my life.	1 2 3 4	I think of others to such an extent that self-denial is becoming the rule rather than the exception in my life.
13. I refuse to get up early to help others.	1 2 3 4	I get up early to help others.
14. I refuse to stay up late to help others.	1 2 3 4	I stay up late to help others.
15. I avoid hard physical labor or crummy jobs.	1 2 3 4	I willingly do hard physical labor or crummy jobs to help others.
16. I compare how much I am doing with how much others are doing.	1 2 3 4	I see that I could never do enough to show my love for God.
17. I complain.	1 2 3 4	I have a thankful attitude.
18. I drag into church or work after being up 'til 2:00 A.M. watching Godzilla V.	1 2 3 4	I prepare to serve so that I'll be able to serve with all my strength.
19. I leave work early to enjoy the weekend.	1 2 3 4	I go the extra mile to make sure my job is done with finesse.
20. I tend to drop out when the newness wears off.	1 2 3 4	I keep going even when I don't see the results I would like.

Rose asked Mrs. Cryan to give her the quiz once a month to help hold her accountable and to help measure her growth. As she grew in being a genuine friend, her lifestyle began to change. She disciplined herself to get to bed early enough so that she wasn't as tempted to hit the snooze button on her alarm repeatedly. That meant she couldn't watch reruns of *Law and Order* anymore; she had to turn off the TV and go to sleep. She also moved her alarm clock across the room so that she would have to get out of bed to shut it off. Rose still struggles to get out of bed but tells herself "Hard is hard; hard is not bad. Yes, it's hard to get out of bed. However, just because it's hard doesn't mean it's bad. God won't give me more than I can handle (1 Corinthians 10:13). I can get up even when it's hard."

She has hidden Proverbs 6:10-11 in her heart to help keep her from sinning when it's time to get out of bed. Her self-talk in the morning often sounds like *"A little sleep, a little slumber, a little folding of the hands to rest—and poverty will come on you like a bandit and scarcity like an armed man."* SHE Asks herself, "Rose, do you want to live in poverty? Then get out of bed."

Rose now arrives at work on time and actually works, rather than chatting with her colleagues for extended periods of time or wasting time on-line. When her boss recently decided he wanted to change protocol for an inventory report Rose produced, Rose simply began learning the new protocol, rather than complaining or pushing back by telling her boss he would have to wait on other projects. Although it did add to Rose's work load, she determined that by arriving at work 15 minutes earlier every day while she was learning the new protocol, she could still get everything done. Even though she'll probably only have to come in early temporarily, Rose would be willing to come early indefinitely. She sees the extra time as restitution for the hours she wasted drinking coffee, chatting with her friends, or doing personal business on work time.

Rose has also been convicted of how much of her employer's time she has wasted in complaining about work. As she looks back, she realizes that she regularly spent 10-15 minutes merely complaining each time she was asked to do something she didn't want to do. Certainly, she was not being any kind of friend to her employer.

While her employer allows employees to take reasonable breaks and develop relationships with co-workers, Rose regularly took advantage of the company's goodness. She used work as her social outlet. Her goal was not to work heartily for her employer; her goal was to get a paycheck. "Don't work too hard," was her often heard parting comment when she finished chatting with a co-worker.

Realizing that genuine friends do not encourage others to make bad choices, Rose now understands that her attitude and actions did not please

God, and that she aided and abetted others in not pleasing God. Like the driver of a get-away car from a bank heist, Rose made it easy for her colleagues and on-line friends to displease God in their jobs.

What Others Experience

For those blessed with genuine friends like Rose, it is easy to delight in the joy of friendship. Like David when he talked about his friends in Psalm 16:3, those who are blessed with genuine friends praise God for His goodness.

Because genuine friends have learned to do their part in the work of the body of believers, the body is able to function better. Those who are gifted as teachers are free to teach without also having to fulfill the duties of an administrator, and gifted administrators can organize without also having to fulfill the duties of a helper. When friends like Rose learn to play their position, the whole body of believers is able to grow and build itself up in love, as each part does its work. Those with servant attitudes enable everyone around them to prosper.

When Rose notices a new person, she takes the initiative to reach out in friendship, even though it moves her out of her comfort zone. She is so concerned that new folks are shown love that she is often among the first people newcomers meet. For visitors, who often feel self-conscious and lonely, Rose's friendliness makes all the difference in the world. Not content to simply introduce herself and then return to her comfort zone, Rose works hard to find common ground to establish a relationship.

As Rose has developed a servant's heart, she rejoices in even the smallest details of serving her friends. Rose does little things to make sure her friends' interests are considered more important than her own. She allows her friends to have aisle seats with the most leg room, she sits behind the tall person in an auditorium so her friends can see, in a restaurant she faces the kitchen, and when they visit Rose her friends find the temperature is set at the level they like. Rather than expecting others to wait on her, Rose is diligent in serving others. Others feel their loads get lighter as a result of Rose's friendship.

Rose is regularly demonstrating that she loves God with all her heart, mind, and strength and that she loves her neighbor as herself.

Chapter 18
From Prestige-Oriented to Genuine
and Authentic Friendships

"Will you marry me?" Receiving a proposal from England's most eligible bachelor is something scripted by reality TV shows and about which most girls only daydream. Marrying a rich man who hangs out with celebrities and politicians would be irresistible to a prestige-oriented friend.

"No," was Florence Nightingale's answer to the proposal of Richard Monckton Milnes, a man purported at the time to be England's most eligible bachelor. Turning her back on wealth and prestige, Florence chose nursing rather than prestige, at a time when nurses were notorious for their immorality. Florence proved she was not a prestige-oriented friend.

A genuine friend, Florence Nightingale led a team of 38 nurses to serve wounded and sick soldiers suffering under appallingly inhumane conditions in the Crimean War. Florence became known as "The Lady with the Lamp" for the way she befriended the wounded soldiers during the night as she made her rounds among them with a lamp in her hand.

Heart's Desire

As we saw in chapter 10, a prestige-oriented friend is very concerned about her reputation. Associating herself, as Florence Nightingale did, with women notorious for being prostitutes and alcoholics would be taboo for a prestige-oriented friend. A genuine and authentic friend, however, is careless of *her* reputation; her zeal is to promote *God's* reputation.

The heart's desire of the prestige-oriented friend who has learned to be genuine and authentic is for God's reputation to be honored. She is very concerned that others have the right opinion of God. She wants God's honor to be high and lifted up.

As a genuine friend there is only one group to which the former prestige-oriented friend wants to belong. She wants to be among those whose names are written in the Book of Life. Far from desiring this to be an exclusive group, the genuine friend would like to see everyone included. She sees herself as a recruiter who wants to advertise available positions in God's family. She is especially sensitive to those who may be overlooked or spurned by others. Her desire is to be a friend of sinners. She delights in seeing those who are shunned or avoided by others come to know the love of Christ.

Acceptable Cost

In order to be a genuine friend, the former prestige-oriented friend is willing to pay the price of being excluded by those who will only associate with individuals who are part of the "in group." As she grows in authentic friendship, she may find that her prestige-oriented friends become less interested in friendship with her. Since the authentic friend isn't trying to climb the ladder of success, she may not be perceived as being able to offer the friendship perks so prized by prestige-oriented friends—entrance into the right circles. No matter. The genuine friend has come to cherish John the Baptist's statement in John 3:30, *"He (Jesus) must become greater; I must become less."*

In the past, the prestige-oriented friend was inclined to believe that God made everyone basically the same, but some could become superior by using their wits and native abilities to climb the success ladder. With this proud attitude, there was little need to be sympathetic to those less fortunate—if they had worked at it, they wouldn't be so unfortunate.

Thus, the poor and underprivileged deserved their plight. The converse was also true. The successful and well-off deserved to be in positions of privilege.

As she repents of her sinful orientation, the deception in the heart of the prestige-oriented friend begins to dissolve. For the first time, the prestige-oriented friend understands 1 Corinthians 4:7: *"For who makes you different from anyone else? What do you have that you did not receive? And if you did receive it, why do you boast as though you did not?"*

Now, rather than adorning herself with pride, she clothes herself with humility. She trades in her necklace of haughtiness for the jewels of humbleness. In so doing, the authentic friend becomes more intimate with God. The authentic friend now experiences God's grace, something she knew little of in the past because God resists the proud, but gives grace to the humble (James 4:6).

Delight/Joy

One of the greatest delights for an authentic friend is to boast about her best friend, God. She realizes she is a wretched sinner saved by God's grace, and she loves to tell others about Him. She wants others to see how amazingly awesome God is.

Sheena, the prestige-oriented friend we met in chapter 10, understands how she formerly replaced God with an idol of prestige. She loves the way Isaiah 44 shows how ludicrous it is to create idols. If you take a piece of wood, carve it into an idol, and then expect that piece of wood to have the power to make all your dreams come true, you are acting foolishly.

In the same way, Sheena has realized how duped she was to create an idol of prestige and expect it to fulfill all her dreams. She believed that being admired by others would bring true happiness, and that holding prominent positions would bring joy. She thought having celebrity status would bring satisfaction. However, the powers she attributed to her idol of prestige were merely something she conjured up in her mind as she became convinced prestige had the power to make her happy. An idol doesn't have the power to do anything.

Sheena has memorized Isaiah 40, in which God is contrasted to idols. Knowing that she has been controlled by an idol of prestige in the past, she wants to arm herself with truth, lest she be tempted to go back to her worship of prestige. She personalized the contrast to make it more vivid for her. In one column she printed the truth of Isaiah 40. In a second column, Sheena adapted the chapter so that it parodies the way she functioned as she worshiped her idol of prestige.

Sheena used the following verses from Isaiah 40 to especially remind her how ridiculous she had been to idolize prestige.

Vs. 9   Call a press conference. Announce to the world, here is your god. Here is **Prestige.**

Vs. 10   See, **Prestige** has all the power; he rules. **Prestige** is the one who gives you rewards.

Vs. 11   **Prestige** cares about you. **Prestige** takes care of you. **Prestige** looks out for you.

Vs. 13   No one is smarter than **Prestige.**

Vs. 18   To whom, then, will you compare **Prestige?**

Vs. 22   **Prestige** sits enthroned above the circle of the earth.

Vs. 23   **Prestige** can make people important or **Prestige** can make them nothing.

Vs. 28   Do you not know? Have you not heard? **Prestige** is the everlasting god, the Creator of the ends of the earth.

Vss. 30   Even youths grow tired and weary, and young men stumble and
-31   fall; but those who hope in **Prestige** will renew their strength. They will soar on wings like eagles; they will run and not grow weary, they will walk and not be faint.

Every time Sheena reviews Isaiah 40, she's reminded not to return to her foolishness.

"Let him who boasts, boast that He knows me," declares the Lord in Jeremiah 9:24. The authentic friend gets this. In the past, the prestige-oriented friend subtly, or not so subtly, boasted about herself and the important friends she knew. Now, her boast is about the God who could redeem someone as proud and prestige-oriented as she has been.

As a natural outcome of exalting God, Sheena delights to honor others more than herself. She looks for ways to make others a success. This genuine friend desires to promote others and she rejoices when others receive honor. In the past, Sheena wanted to be the star performer, now she wants everyone to share in the victory. She promotes unity and teamwork.

Seen in Action

As a prestige-oriented friend, Sheena was all about knowing the right people and belonging to the right groups. As she has grown in becoming a genuine friend, she has become more and more interested in ministering to those who are often neglected by others. She willingly associates with those from any socioeconomic class, but she especially loves those often forgotten or spurned by others. At her church, she serves as a Sunday school assistant to a special needs child. No one who knew Sheena in the past would ever have imagined her humbly assisting a child with toilet skills or allowing a child fixated on her watch to finger it, remove it from her wrist, and examine it. If anyone had left a fingerprint smudge on Sheena's Prada bag in the past, she would have been furious. Now, she doesn't seem to notice the scuffs on her bag after she awkwardly maneuvers the wheelchair of the precious special needs child she serves.

Sheena also participates weekly in her church's prison ministry as a Bible study assistant. She takes a sincere interest in the women who attend and is genuinely distressed to see how the women have been taken captive by sin. She longs for these prisoners to know freedom from the power of sin. Sheena regularly performs acts of service that will never be known by others. Instead of clamoring to achieve the next level of prestige, she views others as more important than herself. Her friends often hear that she has praised them to others.

Sheena struggled for a time in understanding how to have a right view of herself. In the past, she was proud of the skills and abilities she possessed. After she repented, she became disgusted by her pride. As her husband, Anthony, observed Sheena's struggle, he came alongside her to help her begin to have a right view of herself. One evening, he suggested they read Romans 12:3 together.

> ... *Do not think of yourself more highly than you ought, but rather think of yourself with sober judgment in accordance with the measure of faith God has given you.*

After she read it, Sheena confessed, "Anthony, I think I've lived in the first part of that verse most of my life. I've been a living color example of a person who has thought more highly of herself than she ought."

"That's why I wanted us to study Romans 12," responded Anthony. "I don't want to see you go from one ditch to another. I don't want to see you leap from a proud and inflated view of your abilities to a view that you don't have any gifts or abilities God can use.

"As I've watched you grow in humility, it seems to me that you still need to acknowledge the skills God has entrusted to you. I don't want to see you try to squelch your skills and abilities. Romans 12 makes it clear that we have different gifts and that God wants us to use the gifts He has given to strengthen each other.

"Although we shouldn't think more highly of ourselves than we ought, we shouldn't blacken God's name by acting as if He has not blessed us with any abilities. To think of ourselves with sober judgment means we have to recognize the gifts given to us. Failure to do so will prevent us from praising God for His goodness in giving us the gifts and from using them to serve others.

"I think 1 Peter 4:10 would probably be a good summary of this concept. *'Each one should use whatever gift he has received to serve others, faithfully administering God's grace in its various forms.'*"

Anthony also encouraged Sheena to listen to a CD by Lou Priolo in which Priolo described some common misconceptions concerning pride.[71] Sheena took notes and was encouraged by the following list:

- To have a sober understanding of the wisdom, gifts, and abilities which God has given one is not necessarily pride.

- To delight and take pleasure in such wisdom, gifts, and abilities is not necessarily pride.

- To know that certain others are not as wise, gifted, or able in various areas as oneself is not necessarily pride.

---

[71] Priolo, Lou, "How to Help Counselees Who Struggle with Pride" (Workshop given at the 1996 conference of the National Association of Nouthetic Counselors).

- To delight in and value the wisdom God has given one above most everything else is not necessarily pride.

- To rejoice in one's good reputation and the honor that comes with it as long as the rejoicing is based on how such a reputation will glorify God is not necessarily pride.

Sheena's application of these principles is best described by the experience of others who get to know Sheena.

What Others Experience

If you knew Sheena as a prestige-oriented friend, chances are you felt used, you felt as if you had to belong to a certain group in order to be accepted, or you felt excluded and denigrated. All that has changed since Sheena has become a genuine friend. Now, those who experience friendship with Sheena feel loved and warmly accepted. They see her working hard to learn to know them and then using what she learns to minister in meaningful ways. Sheena's humility is very attractive to those in her friendship circle.

One of Sheena's strengths is identifying the skills and abilities of others and encouraging them to maximize their potential. In the past, she evaluated others by how she could use their strengths for her advantage. She still has those powers of observation, but she now uses them to build up the body of Christ, rather than to build up herself.

After she did a friendship U-turn, Sheena began ministering to women who were being released from prison by assisting them in finding jobs. She took the time to assess their skills and then searched out companies that could benefit from an employee with those skills. Never shy about networking with those she believed could help her, Sheena began using her social skills and business contacts with community leaders to help these former prisoners to get back on their feet and become productive employees. Sheena frequently takes vacation days to serve as a job coach to former prisoners who were never taught the skills of being a good employee.

After spending three years connecting former prisoners with job opportunities, Sheena began to understand what it was like to be poor with a prison record. She began to understand the attraction of drugs when she saw the seemingly hopeless life offered to those living in the city projects. She saw 18 year-old girls with three babies trapped in minimum wage jobs. In the lives of these women, the future held no hope, only bleak despair—despair that might be temporarily lifted through a drug high or a fleeting romance likely to end in another pregnancy.

Impassioned by the hopelessness she observed, Sheena began vigorously enlisting others to get involved. Now, five years later, she oversees a job apprenticeship ministry made up of mentors, job coaches, business leaders, and grant writers. More and more businesses have been willing to participate in the apprentice program because of generous grants which help them cover the cost of training, and because of the support they know is provided to help each woman they hire be a successful employee. Most employers have found that their training costs are considerably less than usual and that turnover is lower because of the training and assistance supplied by job coaches.

Recently, Sheena was honored by the city for the job apprenticeship program she helped develop. Leaders from across the city attended the recognition dinner. The award was presented by the governor and reported by several news channels. In her acceptance speech, Sheena passionately described the plight of the women she has come to love, praised the efforts of everyone involved in the ministry, explained opportunities to partner in the ministry, and humbly acknowledged the hand of God in everything, boasting about His ability to lift the needy from the ash heap. That night, rather than anxiously anticipating the 10:00 news, Sheena handwrote over 100 thank you notes to people who had participated in the ministry, acknowledging their contribution, and giving them the appropriate credit for their service. Both Sheena and her husband spent time in prayer, praising God for what He had chosen to do through the ministry.

Sheena no longer resembles a prestige-oriented friend, willing to step on others in order to get to the top. Sheena has become a friend who loves God with all her heart, soul, mind, and strength and a friend who loves others as herself.

Chapter 19
Final Words

Perhaps you started this book with the anticipation that it could offer a few tips on how to have better friendships. Along the way I hope you've come to see that God is interested in much more than simply putting a band-aid on broken relationships. Additionally, God is interested in more than simply restoring relationships to the initial "honeymoon" stage that exists before we realize that the friends we've chosen have significant flaws.

God offers the grace to put together friendships that look like the relationship between God the Father, God the Son, and God the Holy Spirit. These three function in perfect friendship. They praise each other. They are pleased with each other. They don't get peeved with each other. They accomplish great goals together. They have each others' backs. They take pleasure in each other's companionship.

Similarly, God has created us to take pleasure in His companionship and in each others'. In his book, *Heaven*, Randy Alcorn states,

> (In heaven), we'll experience all the best of human rela-
> tionships, with none of the worst. The burdens and trag-

edies of life will be lifted from us. We'll be free of what displeases God and damages relationships. No abortion clinics or psychiatric wards. No missing children. No rape or abuse. No drug rehabilitation centers. No bigotry, muggings, or killings. No worry, depression, or economic downturns. No wars. No unemployment. No anguish over failure and miscommunication. No pretense or wearing masks. No cliques. No hidden agendas, backroom deals, betrayals, secret ambitions, plots, or schemes.

Imagine mealtimes full of stories, laughter, and joy without fear of insensitivity, inappropriate behavior, anger, gossip, lust, jealousy, hurt feelings, or anything that eclipses joy. That will be Heaven.[72]

That will be heaven, but we don't have to wait until heaven to experience sweet unity. Paul Tripp explains this in his book, *Instruments in the Redeemer's Hands*,

> Just before His arrest, Christ prayed for His disciples and those who would believe as a result of their ministry (all of us). In the middle of the prayer, Jesus says,

> John 17:20-23: "My prayer is not for them alone. I pray also for those who will believe in me through their message, that all of them may be one, Father, just as you are in me and I am in you. May they also be in us so that the world may believe that you have sent me. I have given them the glory that you gave me, that they may be one as we are one: I in them and you in me. May they be brought to complete unity to let the world know that you sent me and have loved them even as you have loved me.

> This is a remarkable prayer for a unity comparable only to the Trinity. Jesus prays that His followers would be characterized by such deep love that the community of faith would be as unified as He is with the Father.[73]

---

[72] Alcorn, *Heaven*, p. 367-368.

[73] Tripp, Paul David, *Instruments in the Redeemer's Hands* (Phillipsburg, NJ: P & R Publishing, 2002), p. 101-102.

Notice, Christ clearly expected the unity to occur before heaven. Tripp continues, "(Christ's) prayer also reveals the purpose of this unity. Relationships within the community of faith are meant to reveal the person and work of Christ to a watching world."[74]

So, let's get at it. Let's begin now to enjoy the unity for which Christ prayed, so that the world can see and know Christ! By God's grace and for His glory may you enjoy friendships the way God intended them to be!

---

[74] Ibid, p. 101-102.